LAND O LAKES®
COLLECTOR™ SERIES

Desserts

Double Chocolate Cheesecake With Raspberry Sauce, page 40

Acknowledgments

LAND O LAKES®
COLLECTOR™ SERIES

Russ Moore & Associates, Inc.

Russ Moore, *Publisher*

Richard Cross, *General Manager*

Carla Waldemar, *Executive Editor*

Judy Soranno, *Editor*

Molly Tatting, *Editor*

Nancy McDonough, *Art Director*

Kathleen Keuler Bauwens, *Graphic Design Director*

Kathleen Shaw, *Graphic Designer*

Sue Brosious, *Food Stylist*

Sue Finley, *Food Stylist*

Susan Nielsen, *Production Manager*

Deb Klapperich, *Office Manager*

John W. Kramer, *Director of Sales*

Land O'Lakes, Inc.

Lydia Botham, *Test Kitchens/Consumer Affairs Director*

Becky Wahlund, *Managing Food Editor*

Mary Sue Peterson, *Coordinating Food Editor*

Bob Tenner, *Marketing Director*

Becky Falk, *Marketing Manager*

Tony Kubat Photography

Pictured on front cover: Pumpkin Pecan Layer Cake (page 19)

Recipes developed and tested by the Land O'Lakes Test Kitchens.

LAND O LAKES® Collector™ Series is published by Russ Moore & Associates, Inc., 4151 Knob Drive, St. Paul, MN 55122, 612-452-0571. Direct correspondence to Attention: Publisher, 4151 Knob Drive, St. Paul, MN 55122. Reproduction in whole or part without written permission is prohibited. All rights reserved. ©1993 Land O'Lakes, Inc.

PRINTED IN USA

Desserts

For over 70 years Land O'Lakes has supplied Americans with wholesome and delicious dairy products. It's a name home cooks have learned to trust for quality, and to turn to when planning meals for friends and family.

The Land O'Lakes Test Kitchens also have served as a valued source of new and appealing ways to cook with these popular dairy products. Now we're proud to offer you the best of this heritage of tried and trusted recipes, compiled in an exciting new Collector™ Series. The collection debuts with our favorite subject (and we hope it's yours)—desserts.

From cakes to pies, tarts, cheesecakes and other scrumptious mealtime finales—easy and elegant alike—you'll find plenty of tempting creations that are perfect for any occasion. And they're guaranteed to be delicious. You wouldn't expect anything less from Land O'Lakes.

Just as important: These are recipes you can depend on. Each one has been tested and re-tested by the professional home economists in our Test Kitchens. Each recipe is presented in an easy-to-read, easy-to-follow format to suit the needs of busy modern cooks. And, of course, the nutritional information so important in our lives today also is included. You'll find many traditional favorites to enjoy, along with plenty of fresh, new ideas cooks are looking for—the traditions of tomorrow in the making.

Desserts are the perfect way to end a meal. But for us at Land O'Lakes, they also make a perfect beginning—a great way to launch the new LAND O LAKES® Collector™ Series. Enjoy!

Table of Contents

Table of Contents

Garnishes

To make desserts dazzle, your recipe needs to do more than just taste great—it must look special, too. Here are garnish suggestions that will dress up your desserts for any occasion.

- Flavor 1 cup whipped cream with 1/2 teaspoon extract or 1 tablespoon liqueur, and dollop or pipe with a pastry bag onto pies, cakes, tortes, cheesecakes, etc.

- Chocolate shavings, curls or leaves make attractive garnishes for many desserts.

  - Curls—Warm a bar or block of chocolate in microwave on High until slightly warm (10 to 30 seconds). Using even pressure, pull vegetable peeler across chocolate. (Pressure will determine thickness.) Refrigerate until firm.

  - Leaves—Choose heavy, veined leaves such as lemon or rose leaves. Brush melted chocolate onto undersides of leaves. Refrigerate until firm. Carefully peel leaf away.

- Use holiday cookie cutters as stencils and fill designs with jelly or candy sprinkles to decorate frosted cakes.

- Place paper doily over unfrosted spice, gingerbread or chocolate cake. Sift powdered sugar over doily, then carefully lift off. Cocoa powder can be substituted for powdered sugar on white or yellow cakes.

- Pipe whipped cream or frosting, using a pastry bag or resealable plastic food bag. After filling plastic food bag, take care to snip off only one small corner for piping.

- Dip dried or fresh fruit or nuts into melted white or dark chocolate. Leave green leaves of fruit intact whenever possible.

- Crush candies or use small individual candies or cookies to decorate top or sides of cakes.

Decorative Serving Ideas

To win those "oohs" and "ahs" your dessert creation deserves, showcase it in an attention-getting setting. Here are some decorative serving ideas to add style and color to your presentation.

- Arrange the dessert serving dish or the dessert itself directly on a mirror or mirror tile for a decorative centerpiece.

- Arrange fresh flowers, colorful fall leaves, ribbon or evergreens under a footed dessert dish or plate.

- Place a pie plate inside a grapevine wreath that has been decorated with colorful ribbon, holly or baby's breath.

- Spoon custards or puddings into attractive crystal wine glasses or small water goblets.

- Arrange a cake on a silver or glass tray or plate. Surround with fresh currants, raspberries or cranberries and holly or leaves for a holiday dessert. Or surround with assorted fresh fruits, nuts and evergreens.

- Place a pie plate or pieces of cake in a basket that has been lined with a colorful napkin.

Tortes, Cakes & Cheesecakes

From family favorites
to fancy party fare,
you'll find the perfect
finale here.
Delicate tortes and
tender cakes
that will disappear
in minutes, and
cheesecakes as
easy to make
as they are to enjoy!

Chocolate Mint Layered Torte, page 10

Chocolate Mint Layered Torte

*This elegant four-layer torte can be made with either
chocolate-mint or mocha filling.*

Preparation time: 1 hour 30 minutes • Baking time: 25 minutes • Cooling time: 40 minutes • Chilling time: 1 hour • (pictured on page 8)

Cake
2 cups all-purpose flour
1 1/2 cups sugar
1/2 cup unsweetened cocoa
1/2 cup
  LAND O LAKES® Butter,
  softened
1 cup water
3 eggs
1 1/4 teaspoons baking powder
1 teaspoon baking soda
1 teaspoon vanilla

Filling
2 cups (1 pint) whipping cream
1 1/2 teaspoons mint extract
2 tablespoons sugar

Glaze
2 tablespoons
  LAND O LAKES® Butter
1/2 cup semi-sweet real
  chocolate chips
2 tablespoons light corn syrup
1/4 teaspoon mint extract

Heat oven to 350°. Grease 2 (9-inch) round cake pans. Line each pan with 9-inch round piece of waxed paper; grease waxed paper. Set aside. In large mixer bowl combine all cake ingredients. Beat at medium speed, scraping bowl often, until smooth (2 to 3 minutes). Pour batter into prepared pans. Bake for 20 to 25 minutes or until wooden pick inserted in center comes out clean. Cool 10 minutes; remove from pans. Remove waxed paper; cool completely. In chilled small mixer bowl combine chilled whipping cream and 1 1/2 teaspoons mint extract. Beat at high speed, scraping bowl often, until soft peaks form. Continue beating, gradually adding sugar, until stiff peaks form (1 to 2 minutes). <u>Reserve 1/2 cup filling</u> for garnish; refrigerate.

Using serrated knife, cut each cake layer horizontally in half. To assemble torte, place one split cake layer on serving plate; spread with <u>1/3</u> filling. Repeat with remaining cake layers and filling, ending with cake layer. Refrigerate torte at least 1 hour. In 1-quart saucepan melt 2 tablespoons butter. Stir in chocolate chips and corn syrup. Cook over low heat, stirring constantly, until chocolate chips are melted (2 to 3 minutes). Remove from heat; stir in 1/4 teaspoon mint extract. Spread glaze over top of torte, allowing glaze to drizzle down sides. Garnish with reserved 1/2 cup filling. Refrigerate until ready to serve. **YIELD:** 16 servings.

VARIATION
Chocolate Mocha Torte: <u>Omit 1 1/2 teaspoons mint extract in filling and 1/4 teaspoon mint extract in glaze.</u> Add 3 tablespoons coffee-flavored liqueur to filling and 1 teaspoon coffee-flavored liqueur to glaze.

Nutrition Information (1 serving): Calories 480; Protein 6g; Carbohydrate 52g; Fat 29g; Cholesterol 150mg; Sodium 287mg.

Chocolate Caramel Truffle Torte

Warm caramel sauce is drizzled over this
sinfully rich chocolate torte.

Preparation time: 45 minutes • Baking time: 18 minutes • Cooling time: 30 minutes • Chilling time: 2 hours

Crust

1 3/4 cups very finely chopped
    pecans
2/3 cup sugar
1/4 cup
    LAND O LAKES® Butter,
    melted

Filling

16 ounces high quality
    semi-sweet real chocolate,
    coarsely chopped*
2 cups (1 pint) whipping
    cream

Caramel Sauce

3/4 cup firmly packed
    brown sugar
3/4 cup sugar
1/2 cup light corn syrup
1/3 cup
    LAND O LAKES® Butter
2/3 cup whipping cream

Garnish

1 1/3 cups whipping cream

Heat oven to 350°. In medium bowl stir together all crust ingredients. Firmly press on bottom and up sides of 12-inch tart pan with removable bottom. Place on cookie sheet. Bake for 15 to 18 minutes or until lightly browned. Cool completely. In 2-quart saucepan place 2 cups whipping cream. Cook over medium heat until whipping cream just comes to a boil (5 to 8 minutes). Remove from heat; stir in chocolate until completely melted (2 to 3 minutes). Pour into cooled crust. Refrigerate until set (at least 2 hours). Twenty minutes before serving, in 2-quart saucepan combine all caramel sauce ingredients <u>except</u> 2/3 cup whipping cream. Cook over medium heat, stirring occasionally, until mixture comes to a full boil (5 to 8 minutes). Cool 5 minutes; stir in 2/3 cup whipping cream. Just before serving, in chilled small mixer bowl beat 1 1/3 cups chilled whipping cream at high speed, scraping bowl often, until stiff peaks form (1 to 2 minutes). Garnish torte with whipped cream; serve with warm caramel sauce. **YIELD:** 16 servings.

* 16 ounces (2 2/3 cups) semi-sweet real chocolate chips can be substituted for 16 ounces high quality semi-sweet real chocolate.

TIP: Crust, filling and caramel sauce can be prepared 1 day before serving. Reheat caramel sauce just before serving.

Nutrition Information (1 serving): Calories 630; Protein 4g; Carbohydrate 56g; Fat 47g; Cholesterol 100mg; Sodium 102mg.

Blueberry-Peach Ice Cream Torte

Fresh peaches swirled in ice cream and topped with a blueberry sauce make an elegant presentation.

Preparation time: 1 hour • Freezing time: 12 hours • (pictured)

2 cups (3 medium) fresh
  peaches, peeled, sliced*
2 tablespoons sugar
1 package (12) ladyfingers,
  split
1/2 gallon vanilla ice cream,
  slightly softened

Sauce
1/3 cup sugar
2 tablespoons cornstarch
1 cup water
2 tablespoons
  LAND O LAKES® Butter
2 tablespoons lemon juice
1 teaspoon grated lemon peel
2 cups fresh or frozen blueberries (do not thaw)

In 5-cup blender container combine peach slices and 2 tablespoons sugar. Cover; blend at High speed until well blended (30 to 40 seconds). Set aside. Place split ladyfingers upright (rounded side out) around edge of 10-inch springform pan, fitting closely together. Place ice cream in large bowl. Swirl in peach mixture. Place, by spoonfuls, evenly into prepared pan, pressing gently to level ice cream. Cover with aluminum foil; freeze at least 12 hours or overnight. In 2-quart saucepan combine 1/3 cup sugar and cornstarch; stir in water. Cook over medium heat, stirring occasionally, until mixture thickens and comes to a full boil (3 to 5 minutes). Boil 1 minute. Stir in butter, lemon juice and lemon peel. Cool 10 minutes. Stir in blueberries. Just before serving, pour sauce over top of torte. **YIELD:** 12 servings.

*2 cups frozen sliced peaches, thawed, can be substituted for 2 cups fresh peaches.

TIP: 9-inch round cake pan can be substituted for 10-inch springform pan. Line with aluminum foil, extending excess aluminum foil over edges. After torte is frozen, lift torte from pan, using aluminum foil as handles. Remove aluminum foil.

TIP: Fresh blueberries make a clear sauce; frozen blueberries make a blueberry-colored sauce.

Nutrition Information (1 serving): Calories 300; Protein 4g; Carbohydrate 44g; Fat 12g; Cholesterol 84mg; Sodium 105mg.

Raspberry Crowned Chocolate Torte

A rich brownie-like torte is topped with glistening raspberry preserves and garnished with whipped cream.

Preparation time: 1 hour • Baking time: 55 minutes • Cooling time: 1 hour • Chilling time: 3 hours • (pictured)

3 eggs, separated

1/8 teaspoon cream of tartar

1/8 teaspoon salt

1 1/2 cups sugar

1 cup
   LAND O LAKES® Butter,
   melted

1 1/2 teaspoons vanilla

1/2 cup all-purpose flour

1/2 cup unsweetened cocoa

3 tablespoons water

3/4 cup finely chopped
   almonds

1/3 cup raspberry preserves

Sweetened whipped cream

Fresh raspberries

Heat oven to 350°. Grease 9-inch round cake pan. Line with aluminum foil, leaving excess foil over edges; grease foil. Set aside. In small mixer bowl combine egg whites, cream of tartar and salt. Beat at high speed, scraping bowl often, until soft peaks form (1 to 2 minutes); set aside. In large mixer bowl combine egg yolks, sugar, butter and vanilla. Beat at medium speed, scaping bowl often, until well mixed (1 to 2 minutes). Add flour, cocoa and water. Continue beating, scraping bowl often, until well mixed (1 to 2 minutes). Stir in chopped almonds. Fold beaten egg whites into chocolate mixture. Spread into prepared pan. Bake for 40 to 55 minutes or until firm to the touch. (Do not overbake.) Cool on wire rack 1 hour; remove from pan by lifting aluminum foil. Cover; refrigerate until completely cooled (2 to 3 hours). Remove aluminum foil; place on serving plate. Spread raspberry preserves on top. Garnish with sweetened whipped cream and raspberries. **YIELD:** 12 servings.

Nutrition Information (1 serving): Calories 350; Protein 5g; Carbohydrate 38g; Fat 22g; Cholesterol 111mg; Sodium 226mg.

Special Occasion Layer Cake

*Creme de cacao, chocolate butter cream and white chocolate frosting
combine to make this three-tier cake perfect for special occasions.*

Preparation time: 1 hour • Baking time: 25 minutes • Cooling time: 35 minutes • (pictured)

Cake

2 cups all-purpose flour

1 1/2 cups sugar

1/2 cup
   LAND O LAKES® Butter,
   softened

1 cup milk

4 egg whites

3 1/2 teaspoons baking powder

1/2 teaspoon salt

1 teaspoon vanilla

6 tablespoons creme de cacao

Filling

1/2 cup powdered sugar

1/4 cup
   LAND O LAKES® Butter,
   softened

1 (1 ounce) square unsweetened baking chocolate,
   melted, cooled

1 tablespoon whipping cream

Frosting

2 cups powdered sugar

1/4 cup
   LAND O LAKES® Butter,
   softened

3 ounces white chocolate,
   melted, cooled

4 to 5 tablespoons whipping
   cream

White & dark chocolate leaves

Heat oven to 350°. In large mixer bowl combine all cake ingredients <u>except</u> creme de cacao. Beat at low speed, scraping bowl often, until all ingredients are moistened. Beat at high speed, scraping bowl often, until smooth (3 to 4 minutes). Pour into 3 greased and floured 8-inch round cake pans. Bake for 20 to 25 minutes or until wooden pick inserted in center comes out clean. Cool 5 minutes; remove from pans. Cool completely. In small mixer bowl combine all filling ingredients. Beat at high speed, scraping bowl often, until light and fluffy (2 to 3 minutes); set aside. In small mixer bowl combine all frosting ingredients. Beat at high speed, scraping bowl often, until light and fluffy (2 to 3 minutes). To assemble cake, place 1 layer on serving plate. Poke top of cake all over with fork; sprinkle with <u>2 tablespoons</u> creme de cacao. Spread with <u>1/2</u> filling. Place second cake layer on top. Poke top of cake all over with fork; sprinkle with <u>2 tablespoons</u> creme de cacao. Spread with remaining filling. Place third cake layer on top. Poke top of cake all over with fork; sprinkle with <u>2 tablespoons</u> creme de cacao. Frost entire cake with frosting. If desired, garnish with chocolate leaves. **YIELD:** 12 servings.

TIP: 3 (9-inch) round cake pans can be substituted for 3 (8-inch) round cake pans. Bake for 15 to 20 minutes or until wooden pick inserted in center comes out clean.

Nutrition Information (1 serving): Calories 510; Protein 5g; Carbohydrate 75g; Fat 22g; Cholesterol 54mg; Sodium 374mg.

Icebox Banana Cake With Chocolate Cream

This cake tastes great right from the refrigerator,
or it freezes beautifully for a chilled treat.

Preparation time: 1 hour • Baking time: 30 minutes • Cooling time: 30 minutes • Chilling time: 2 hours

Cake

1 cup sugar

2/3 cup
   LAND O LAKES® Butter,
   softened

2 teaspoons vanilla

2 eggs

1 cup (2 medium) mashed ripe
   bananas

1/4 cup LAND O LAKES®
   Light Sour Cream
   or dairy sour cream

1 1/2 cups all-purpose flour

1 teaspoon baking soda

Chocolate Cream

1 1/2 cups whipping cream

3 tablespoons powdered sugar

1 teaspoon vanilla

1/2 cup semi-sweet real
   chocolate chips, melted

2 bananas

2 tablespoons chopped pecans

Heat oven to 350°. In large mixer bowl combine sugar, butter and 2 teaspoons vanilla. Beat at low speed, scraping bowl often, until light and fluffy (1 to 2 minutes). Continue beating, adding eggs one at a time, until creamy (1 to 2 minutes). By hand, stir in 1 cup mashed bananas and Light Sour Cream. Fold in flour and baking soda. Pour into 2 greased and floured 8-inch round cake pans. Bake for 25 to 30 minutes or until wooden pick inserted in center comes out clean. Cool 5 minutes; remove from pans. Cool completely.

In chilled small mixer bowl beat chilled whipping cream at high speed, scraping bowl often, until soft peaks form. Continue beating, gradually adding sugar and 1 teaspoon vanilla, until stiff peaks form (1 to 2 minutes). Add melted chocolate; continue beating until well mixed (1 minute). (Do not overbeat.) On serving plate, place 1 cake layer. Spread with half of chocolate cream. Slice 1 banana; lay banana slices on top of chocolate cream. Top with remaining cake layer. Frost top of cake with remaining chocolate cream. Refrigerate or freeze cake 2 hours or overnight. To serve, slice remaining banana; arrange banana slices around outside edge of cake. Sprinkle pecans in center of cake. Serve immediately or freeze to prevent bananas from browning. **YIELD:** 12 servings.

TIP: 2 (9-inch) round cake pans can be substituted for 2 (8-inch) round cake pans. Bake for 20 to 25 minutes.

Nutrition Information (1 serving): Calories 420; Protein 4g; Carbohydrate 45g; Fat 26g; Cholesterol 105mg; Sodium 220mg.

Pumpkin Pecan Layer Cake

*Three layers of festive fall flavors create
this memorable cake.*

Preparation time: 45 minutes • Baking time: 25 minutes • Cooling time: 30 minutes • (pictured on cover)

Cake

2 cups crushed vanilla wafers

1 cup chopped pecans

3/4 cup
  LAND O LAKES® Butter,
  softened

1 (18 ounce) package spice
  cake mix

1 (16 ounce) can pumpkin

1/4 cup
  LAND O LAKES® Butter,
  softened

4 eggs

Filling

3 cups powdered sugar

2/3 cup
  LAND O LAKES® Butter,
  softened

4 ounces cream cheese,
  softened

2 teaspoons vanilla

1/4 cup caramel topping

1 cup pecan halves

Heat oven to 350°. In large mixer bowl combine wafer crumbs, chopped pecans and 3/4 cup butter. Beat at medium speed, scraping bowl often, until crumbly (1 to 2 minutes). Press mixture evenly on bottom of 3 greased and floured 9-inch round cake pans. In same bowl combine cake mix, pumpkin, 1/4 cup butter and eggs. Beat at medium speed, scraping bowl often, until well mixed (2 or 3 minutes). Spread <u>1 3/4 cups</u> batter over crumbs in each pan. Bake for 20 to 25 minutes or until wooden pick inserted in center comes out clean. Cool 5 minutes; remove from pans. Cool completely. In small mixer bowl combine powdered sugar, 2/3 cup butter, cream cheese and vanilla. Beat at medium speed, scraping bowl often, until light and fluffy (2 to 3 minutes). On serving plate layer 3 cakes, nut side down, with <u>1/2 cup</u> filling spread between each layer. With remaining filling, frost sides only of cake. Spread caramel topping over top of cake, drizzling some over frosted sides. Arrange pecan halves in rings on top of cake. Store refrigerated.
YIELD: 16 servings.

TIP: To remove cake easily from pan, place wire rack on top of cake and invert; repeat with remaining layers.

Nutrition Information (1 serving): Calories 600; protein 22g; Carbohydrate 60g; Fat 38g; Cholesterol 123mg; Sodium 490mg.

Chocolate Sponge Cake With Fresh Fruit

This unique mixture of chocolate and fruit
is perfect for any season.

Preparation time: 45 minutes • Baking time: 23 minutes • Cooling time: 30 minutes • (pictured)

Cake

1 cup powdered sugar

4 eggs, room temperature

1 egg yolk, room temperature

1 tablespoon creme de cacao*

1/2 cup all-purpose flour

1/4 cup Dutch process cocoa <u>or</u>
   unsweetened cocoa

1/8 teaspoon salt

2 tablespoons
   LAND O LAKES® Butter,
   melted

Topping

1 pint strawberries, hulled, cut
   in half

1 kiwi, peeled, sliced 1/8-inch,
   cut in half

1/2 cup fresh raspberries

1/2 cup fresh blueberries

1 (10 ounce) jar apple jelly,
   heated until liquid

Sweetened whipped cream

Heat oven to 375°. Grease and flour 10-inch removable-bottom tart pan. Place pan on cookie sheet; set aside. In large mixer bowl combine powdered sugar, eggs, egg yolk and creme de cacao. Beat at high speed, scraping bowl often, until mixture is very thick and double in volume (5 to 8 minutes). (Mixture should be light yellow and consistency of soft whipped cream.) In medium bowl sift together flour, cocoa and salt. By hand, gently fold flour mixture into egg mixture just until flour is moistened. Fold butter into batter. Gently spoon batter into prepared pan. Bake for 20 to 23 minutes or until wooden pick inserted in center comes out clean. Cool completely on wire rack. To serve, decoratively arrange fresh fruit on top of cake. Drizzle warm jelly over top of cake and fruit. Garnish with sweetened whipped cream. **YIELD:** 12 servings.

*1 teaspoon vanilla can be substituted for 1 tablespoon creme de cacao.

Nutrition Information (1 serving): Calories 190; Protein 4g; Carbohydrate 35g; Fat 5g; Cholesterol 95mg; Sodium 80mg.

Chocolate Chip Macaroon Angel Food

Homemade angel food cake, light as a cloud
and worth the extra effort.

Preparation time: 1 hour • Baking time: 35 minutes • Cooling time: 1 hour 30 minutes

Cake

1 1/2 cups powdered sugar

1 cup cake flour*

1 1/2 cups (about 12) egg
    whites

1 1/2 teaspoons cream of tartar

1 cup sugar

1/4 teaspoon salt

1 teaspoon almond extract

1 teaspoon vanilla

1 cup mini semi-sweet
    chocolate chips

1/2 cup flaked coconut

2 cups sweetened whipped
    cream

1 cup toasted flaked coconut

Heat oven to 375°. In small bowl stir together powdered sugar and flour; set aside. In large mixer bowl beat egg whites and cream of tartar at medium speed until foamy (1 to 2 minutes). Beat at high speed, gradually adding 1 cup sugar, 2 tablespoons at a time. Continue beating, adding salt, almond extract and vanilla and scraping bowl often, until stiff and glossy (6 to 8 minutes). By hand, gradually fold in flour mixture, 1/4 cup at a time. Fold in just until flour mixture disappears. Fold in chocolate chips and 1/2 cup coconut. Spread batter into 10-inch tube pan. Cut gently through batter with metal spatula. Bake for 30 to 35 minutes or until cracks feel dry and top springs back when touched lightly. Invert pan on heat-proof funnel or bottle; let cool 1 1/2 hours. Remove from pan. De-crumb cake with fingertips. Place cake on serving plate. Pipe top and around bottom of cake with sweetened whipped cream; sprinkle with toasted coconut. **YIELD:** 16 servings.

*1 cup minus 2 tablespoons all-purpose flour can be substituted for 1 cup
  cake flour.

TIP: 1 (16 ounce) package angel food cake mix can be substituted for homemade cake.

Nutrition Information (1 serving): Calories 270; Protein 4g; Carbohydrate 39g; Fat 12g;
Cholesterol 20mg; Sodium 85mg

Pineapple Filled Jelly Roll

Pineapple filling adds a wonderful new taste
to a traditional jelly roll.

Preparation time: 45 minutes • Baking time: 15 minutes • Cooling time: 30 minutes • Chilling time: 3 hours

Cake

4 eggs, separated
3/4 cup sugar
1 teaspoon baking powder
1/4 teaspoon salt
1/2 teaspoon vanilla
1/2 cup all-purpose flour

Powdered sugar

Filling

1/2 cup firmly packed brown
   sugar
1/4 cup
   LAND O LAKES® Butter
1 (20 ounce) can crushed
   pineapple in syrup, drained,
   reserve syrup
1/2 cup reserved pineapple
   syrup
1 tablespoon cornstarch

Powdered sugar
Sweetened whipped cream
Maraschino cherries

Heat oven to 375°. Grease 15x10x1-inch jelly roll pan. Line with waxed paper; grease waxed paper. Set aside. In small mixer bowl beat egg whites at high speed until foamy. Continue beating, gradually adding 1/4 cup sugar, until stiff peaks form (2 to 3 minutes); set aside. In large mixer bowl combine egg yolks, remaining 1/2 cup sugar, baking powder, salt and vanilla. Beat at medium speed, scraping bowl often, until well mixed (1 to 2 minutes). Alternately fold in egg whites and flour until just mixed. Pour into prepared pan. Bake for 10 to 15 minutes or until top springs back when lightly touched.

Immediately loosen cake from edges of pan. Invert onto towel sprinkled with powdered sugar. Remove pan; peel off waxed paper. While hot, starting with 10-inch side, roll up cake in towel. Cool completely. In 2-quart saucepan combine all filling ingredients. Cook over medium heat, stirring occasionally, until mixture comes to a full boil (8 to 10 minutes); boil 1 minute. Refrigerate until completely cooled (2 to 3 hours). Unroll cooled cake; remove towel. Spread cake with cooled filling; roll up cake. Refrigerate until ready to serve. If desired, garnish with powdered sugar, whipped cream and cherries. **YIELD:** 10 servings.

Nutrition Information (1 serving): Calories 240; Protein 3g; Carbohydrate 43g; Fat 7g; Cholesterol 98mg; Sodium 160 mg.

Lemon Poppy Seed Pound Cake

*Lemon complements the rich, moist flavor of
this delicate cake.*

Preparation time: 30 minutes • Baking time: 65 minutes • Cooling time: 1 hour 30 minutes • (pictured)

Cake

3 cups all-purpose flour

2 cups sugar

1/4 cup poppy seed

1 cup
   LAND O LAKES® Butter,
   softened

1 cup buttermilk*

4 eggs

1/2 teaspoon baking soda

1/2 teaspoon baking powder

1/2 teaspoon salt

4 teaspoons grated lemon peel

1/2 teaspoon vanilla

Glaze

1 cup powdered sugar

1 to 2 tablespoons lemon juice

Heat oven to 325°. In large mixer bowl combine all cake ingredients. Beat at low speed, scraping bowl often, until all ingredients are moistened. Beat at high speed, scraping bowl often, until smooth (1 to 2 minutes). Pour into greased and floured 12-cup Bundt pan or 10-inch tube pan. Bake for 55 to 65 minutes or until wooden pick inserted in center comes out clean. Cool 10 minutes; remove from pan. Cool completely. In small bowl stir together powdered sugar and lemon juice until smooth. Drizzle over cake. **YIELD:** 16 servings.

*1 tablespoon vinegar plus enough milk to equal 1 cup can be substituted for 1 cup buttermilk.

Nutrition Information (1 serving): Calories 340; Protein 5g; Carbohydrate 51g; Fat 14g; Cholesterol 85mg; Sodium 260mg.

Spiced Carrot Cake With Vanilla Sauce

*Tender and moist spiced carrot cake is
served with a warm vanilla sauce.*

Preparation time: 1 hour 15 minutes • Baking time: 45 minutes

Cake

1 1/3 cups all-purpose flour

1/3 cup sugar

1/2 cup
  LAND O LAKES® Butter,
  softened

1/2 cup orange juice

2 eggs

1 teaspoon baking powder

1 teaspoon baking soda

1 teaspoon cinnamon

1/2 teaspoon nutmeg

1/4 teaspoon salt

1 cup (2 medium) shredded
  carrots

3/4 cup raisins

Sauce

1/3 cup
  LAND O LAKES® Butter

1/3 cup sugar

2 tablespoons cornstarch

1 1/2 cups half-and-half

2 teaspoons vanilla

Heat oven to 325°. In large mixer bowl combine all cake ingredients <u>except</u> carrots and raisins. Beat at medium speed, scraping bowl often, until well mixed (1 to 2 minutes). By hand, stir in carrots and raisins. Pour into greased 6-cup Bundt pan or cake mold. Bake for 35 to 45 minutes or until cake begins to pull away from sides of pan. Cool 5 minutes; remove from pan. Meanwhile, in 2-quart saucepan melt 1/3 cup butter. Stir in 1/3 cup sugar and cornstarch; add remaining sauce ingredients. Cook over medium heat, stirring occasionally, until sauce comes to a full boil (5 to 7 minutes). Boil 1 minute. Pour <u>1/4 cup</u> sauce over cake; serve additional warm sauce with cake. **YIELD:** 8 servings.

TIP: Cake can be baked in a greased 8-inch square baking pan. Bake for 20 to 25 minutes or until cake begins to pull away from the side of pan.

Nutrition Information (1 serving): Calories 450; Protein 6g; Carbohydrate 51g; Fat 26g; Cholesterol 122mg; Sodium 480mg.

Orange Chocolate Creme Cake

Orange frosting complements this
chocolate sour cream cake.

Preparation time: 45 minutes • Baking time: 45 minutes • Cooling time: 1 hour

Cake

2 cups all-purpose flour

1 1/2 cups sugar

1 teaspoon baking soda

1 teaspoon baking powder

1 teaspoon salt

4 (1 ounce) squares
   unsweetened baking
   chocolate, melted

1 cup orange juice

3/4 cup LAND O LAKES®
   Light Sour Cream
   or dairy sour cream

1/2 cup
   LAND O LAKES® Butter,
   softened

2 eggs

1 1/2 teaspoons grated
   orange peel

Frosting

2 cups powdered sugar

1/4 cup
   LAND O LAKES® Butter,
   softened

1/4 cup LAND O LAKES®
   Light Sour Cream
   or dairy sour cream

2 teaspoons orange juice

1/2 teaspoon grated
   orange peel

1 (1 ounce) square unsweetened
   baking chocolate, melted

Heat oven to 350°. In large mixer bowl combine all cake ingredients. Beat at medium speed, scraping bowl often, until smooth (2 to 3 minutes). Pour into greased and floured 13x9-inch baking pan. Bake for 35 to 45 minutes or until top springs back when touched lightly in center. Cool completely. In small mixer bowl combine all frosting ingredients except chocolate. Beat at medium speed, scraping bowl often, until light and fluffy (1 to 2 minutes). Frost cooled cake. Drizzle top with melted chocolate. **YIELD:** 15 servings.

Nutrition Information (1 serving): Calories 360; Protein 4g; Carbohydrate 53g; Fat 16g; Cholesterol 55mg; Sodium 350mg.

Chocolate Rocky Road Cake

Chocolate, marshmallows and peanuts
top this moist chocolate cake.

Preparation time: 45 minutes • Baking time: 42 minutes • (pictured)

Cake

2 cups all-purpose flour
1 1/2 cups sugar
1/2 cup unsweetened cocoa
1/2 cup
   LAND O LAKES® Butter,
   softened
1 cup water
3 eggs
1 1/4 teaspoons baking powder
1 teaspoon baking soda
1 teaspoon vanilla

Frosting

2 cups miniature
   marshmallows

1/4 cup
   LAND O LAKES® Butter
1 (3 ounce) package cream
   cheese
1 (1 ounce) square unsweetened
   baking chocolate
2 tablespoons milk
3 cups powdered sugar
1 teaspoon vanilla

1/2 cup coarsely chopped
   salted peanuts

Heat oven to 350°. In large mixer bowl combine all cake ingredients. Beat at low speed, scraping bowl often, until ingredients are moistened. Beat at high speed, scraping bowl often, until smooth (1 to 2 minutes). Pour into greased and floured 13x9-inch baking pan. Bake for 30 to 40 minutes or until wooden pick inserted in center comes out clean. Sprinkle with marshmallows. Continue baking 2 minutes or until marshmallows are softened. Meanwhile, in 2-quart saucepan combine 1/4 cup butter, cream cheese, chocolate and milk. Cook over medium heat, stirring occasionally, until melted (8 to 10 minutes). Remove from heat; stir in powdered sugar and vanilla until smooth. Pour over marshmallows and swirl together. Sprinkle with peanuts.
YIELD: 15 servings.

Nutrition Information (1 serving): Calories 400; Protein 6g; Carbohydrate 61g; Fat 16g; Cholesterol 75mg; Sodium 290mg.

Chocolate Chip Pound Cake Squares

*A dessert that is reminiscent of old-fashioned pound cake
with a sauce that's a chocolate dream.*

Preparation time: 20 minutes • Baking time: 35 minutes

Cake

1 cup sugar

2/3 cup
  LAND O LAKES® Butter,
  softened

3 eggs

1 1/4 cups all-purpose flour

1/2 cup miniature semi-sweet
  real chocolate chips

1 tablespoon vanilla

Sauce

1 cup miniature semi-sweet
  real chocolate chips

1/2 cup whipping cream

Heat oven to 350°. In large mixer bowl combine sugar and butter. Beat at low speed, scraping bowl often, until light and fluffy (1 to 2 minutes). Continue beating, adding eggs one at a time, until creamy (1 to 2 minutes). By hand, fold in all remaining cake ingredients. Pour into greased 9-inch square baking pan. Bake for 30 to 35 minutes or until wooden pick inserted in center comes out clean. In 1-quart saucepan place 1 cup chocolate chips and whipping cream. Cook over low heat, stirring constantly, until chocolate is melted (4 to 6 minutes). Serve sauce over squares. **YIELD:** 9 servings.

Nutrition Information (1 serving): Calories 480; Protein 5g; Carbohydrate 52g; Fat 31g; Cholesterol 126mg; Sodium 170mg.

Apple Crisp Cake With Rum Sauce

*Not apple crisp, not apple cake, but a combination ——
topped with a rum-flavored sauce.*

Preparation time: 45 minutes • Baking time: 40 minutes

Topping
1/3 cup all-purpose flour
1/3 cup quick-cooking oats
1/4 cup firmly packed brown
   sugar
1/4 cup LAND O LAKES®
   Butter, softened

Cake
1 cup all-purpose flour
1/2 cup sugar
1/2 cup LAND O LAKES®
   Light Sour Cream
   <u>or</u> dairy sour cream
1/4 cup
   LAND O LAKES® Butter,
   softened
1 egg
1 teaspoon cinnamon
1/2 teaspoon baking powder
1/2 teaspoon baking soda
1/4 teaspoon salt
1/2 cup chopped pecans

2 cups (2 medium) peeled,
   cored, sliced 1/8-inch,
   cut in half tart cooking apples

Sauce
1/3 cup sugar
1/3 cup firmly packed brown
   sugar
1/4 cup
   LAND O LAKES® Butter
1/4 cup light corn syrup
1/3 cup whipping cream
1/2 teaspoon rum extract

Cream, sweetened whipped
   cream <u>or</u> vanilla ice cream

Heat oven to 375°. In small mixer bowl combine all topping ingredients. Beat at low speed, scraping bowl often, until crumbly (1 to 2 minutes); set aside. In large mixer bowl combine all cake ingredients <u>except</u> pecans and apples. Beat at medium speed, scraping bowl often, until well mixed (2 to 3 minutes). By hand, stir in pecans. Spread into greased 9-inch square baking pan. Arrange apple slices in rows on top of batter. Sprinkle with reserved topping. Bake for 35 to 40 minutes or until topping is golden brown and apples are fork tender. Meanwhile, in 1-quart saucepan combine all sauce ingredients <u>except</u> whipping cream and rum extract. Cook over medium heat, stirring occasionally, until mixture comes to a full boil (6 to 10 minutes). Cool 5 minutes. Stir in 1/3 cup whipping cream and rum extract. Serve warm rum sauce over cake. If desired, top with cream, sweetened whipped cream or ice cream. **YIELD:** 9 servings.

*Nutrition Information (1 serving): Calories 480; Protein 5g; Carbohydrate 62g; Fat 25g;
Cholesterol 81mg; Sodium 330mg.*

Honey Spice Cake With Orange Cream

*A light and creamy orange topping adds a delightful touch
to a homemade spice cake.*

Preparation time: 45 minutes • Baking time: 40 minutes • (pictured)

Cake

1/2 cup firmly packed brown
   sugar
1/4 cup
   LAND O LAKES® Butter,
   softened
1/3 cup LAND O LAKES®
   Light Sour Cream
   <u>or</u> dairy sour cream
1/3 cup orange juice
1/4 cup honey
2 egg whites
2 cups all-purpose flour
1 teaspoon baking soda
1 teaspoon cinnamon
1/2 teaspoon ginger
1/4 teaspoon salt

Orange Cream

2/3 cup LAND O LAKES®
   Light Sour Cream
   <u>or</u> dairy sour cream
1 tablespoon sugar
1 teaspoon grated orange peel
1 tablespoon orange juice

Heat oven to 325°. In large mixer bowl combine brown sugar, butter, 1/3 cup Light Sour Cream, 1/3 cup orange juice, honey and egg whites. Beat at low speed, scraping bowl often, until well mixed (1 to 2 minutes). Continue beating, gradually adding all remaining cake ingredients, until well mixed (1 to 2 minutes). Pour into greased 9-inch round cake pan. Bake for 35 to 40 minutes or until wooden pick inserted in center comes out clean. Meanwhile, in small bowl stir together all orange cream ingredients. Serve cake warm or cool with dollop of orange cream. **YIELD:** 10 servings.

*Nutrition Information (1 serving): Calories 240; Protein 4g; Carbohydrate 42g; Fat 6g;
Cholesterol 18mg; Sodium 250mg.*

Harvest Time Cake

*This hearty cake is chock-full of delightful extras
like pecans, raisins and apples.*

Preparation time: 1 hour • Baking time: 50 minutes • Cooling time: 1 hour

Cake

3 cups all-purpose flour
1 3/4 cups sugar
1 tablespoon baking soda
1 tablespoon cinnamon
1/2 teaspoon salt
1 1/4 cups
  LAND O LAKES® Butter,
  melted
4 eggs
1 tablespoon vanilla
3 cups (6 medium) grated
  carrots
1 cup (1 large) peeled, grated
  apple
1 cup chopped pecans
1/2 cup raisins
1/2 cup flaked coconut

Frosting

1/3 cup
  LAND O LAKES® Butter
3 cups powdered sugar
1 1/2 teaspoons vanilla
2 to 4 tablespoons milk

Heat oven to 350°. In large bowl combine flour, sugar, baking soda, cinnamon and salt. Stir in 1 1/4 cups butter, eggs and 1 tablespoon vanilla until well mixed. Stir in all remaining cake ingredients. Pour into greased 13x9-inch baking pan. Bake for 40 to 50 minutes or until wooden pick inserted in center comes out clean. Cool completely. In 1-quart saucepan heat 1/3 cup butter over medium heat until delicate brown (5 to 6 minutes). In small mixer bowl combine browned butter, powdered sugar and 1 1/2 teaspoons vanilla. Beat at medium speed, scraping bowl often and gradually adding milk, until frosting is smooth and spreadable. Frost cooled cake.

YIELD: 15 servings.

*Nutrition Information (1 serving): Calories 540; Protein 6g; Carbohydrate 73g; Fat 27g;
Cholesterol 110mg; Sodium 520mg.*

Scrumptious Chocolate Peanut Cake

*A delightful chocolate cake topped with
chocolate chips and peanuts.*

Preparation time: 45 minutes • Baking time: 40 minutes • Cooling time: 1 hour

Cake

2 cups all-purpose flour

1 1/2 cups sugar

1/2 cup unsweetened cocoa

1/2 cup
  LAND O LAKES® Butter,
  softened

1 cup water

3 eggs

1 1/4 teaspoons baking powder

1 teaspoon baking soda

1 teaspoon vanilla

1 cup miniature semi-sweet
  chocolate chips

Frosting

2/3 cup
  LAND O LAKES® Butter,
  softened

1/3 cup peanut butter

4 cups powdered sugar

4 to 5 tablespoons half-and-half
  or milk

1 cup miniature semi-sweet
  chocolate chips

1/2 cup chopped salted peanuts

Heat oven to 350°. In large mixer bowl combine all cake ingredients. Beat at low speed, scraping bowl often, until all ingredients are moistened. Beat at high speed, scraping bowl often, until well mixed (1 to 2 minutes). Pour into greased and floured 13x9-inch baking pan. Bake for 30 to 40 minutes or until wooden pick inserted in center comes out clean; cool completely. In medium bowl combine 2/3 cup butter and peanut butter. Beat at high speed, scraping bowl often, until light and fluffy (1 to 2 minutes). Add powdered sugar. Continue beating on low speed, scraping bowl often and adding half-and-half as needed, until creamy (1 to 2 minutes). Frost top of cake; sprinkle with 1 cup chocolate chips and peanuts. **YIELD:** 20 servings.

Nutrition Information (1 serving): Calories 430; Protein 5g; Carbohydrate 57g; Fat 22g; Cholesterol 60mg; Sodium 260mg.

Buttery Coconut Pecan Cake

This moist cake is topped with an old-fashioned browned butter frosting.

Preparation time: 1 hour • Baking time: 50 minutes • Cooling time: 1 hour • (pictured)

Cake

2 cups all-purpose flour

2 cups sugar

1 1/2 cups
    LAND O LAKES® Butter,
    softened

1 cup buttermilk*

4 eggs

1 teaspoon baking soda

1/2 teaspoon salt

1 tablespoon vanilla

2 cups flaked coconut

1 cup chopped pecans

Frosting

1/3 cup
    LAND O LAKES® Butter

3 cups powdered sugar

1 1/2 teaspoons vanilla

1 to 3 tablespoons milk

Heat oven to 350°. In large mixer bowl combine all cake ingredients <u>except</u> coconut and pecans. Beat at low speed, scraping bowl often, until all ingredients are moistened. Beat at high speed, scraping bowl often, until smooth (3 to 4 minutes). By hand, stir in coconut and pecans. Pour into greased and floured 13x9-inch baking pan. Bake for 45 to 50 minutes or until center of cake is firm to the touch and edges begin to pull away from sides of pan. Cool completely. In 1-quart saucepan heat 1/3 cup butter over medium heat, stirring constantly, until delicate brown (5 to 6 minutes). In small mixer bowl combine melted butter, powdered sugar and vanilla. Beat at medium speed, gradually adding milk and scraping bowl often, until frosting is smooth and spreadable. Frost cooled cake.
YIELD: 15 servings.

*1 tablespoon vinegar plus enough milk to equal 1 cup can be substituted for 1 cup buttermilk.

Nutrition Information (1 serving): Calories 570; Protein 5g; Carbohydrate 66g; Fat 33g; Cholesterol 135mg; Sodium 415mg.

Sweetheart Cheesecake

Rich homemade cheesecake is sweetened with a decorative ring of hearts.

Preparation time: 1 hour • Baking time: 1 hour 30 minutes • Cooling time: 2 hours • Chilling time: 4 hours • (pictured)

Crust

1 1/3 cups crushed chocolate
   wafer cookies
1/4 cup
   LAND O LAKES® Butter,
   melted
2 tablespoons sugar

Filling

4 eggs, separated
1/2 cup
   LAND O LAKES® Butter,
   softened
2 (8 ounce) packages cream
   cheese, softened
1 cup sugar
1 tablespoon cornstarch
1 teaspoon baking powder
1 tablespoon lemon juice

Topping

1 (8 ounce) carton (1 cup)
   LAND O LAKES®
   Light Sour Cream
   or dairy sour cream
2 tablespoons sugar
1 teaspoon vanilla

1 (21 ounce) can cherry
   pie filling
3 tablespoons cherry-flavored
   liqueur, if desired

Heat oven to 325°. In small bowl stir together all crust ingredients. Press crumb mixture evenly onto bottom of 9-inch springform pan. Bake 10 minutes; cool. In small mixer bowl beat egg whites at high speed, scraping bowl often, until soft peaks form (1 to 2 minutes); set aside. In large mixer bowl combine 1/2 cup butter, cream cheese and egg yolks. Beat at medium speed, scraping bowl often, until smooth and creamy (2 to 3 minutes). Add all remaining filling ingredients <u>except</u> egg whites. Continue beating, scraping bowl often, until well mixed (1 to 2 minutes). By hand, fold in beaten egg whites. Spoon filling into prepared pan. Bake for 60 to 80 minutes or until center is set and firm to the touch. (Cheesecake surface will be cracked.)

Cool 15 minutes; loosen sides of cheesecake from pan by running knife around inside of pan. Cool completely. (Cheesecake center will dip slightly upon cooling.) In small bowl stir together Light Sour Cream, 2 tablespoons sugar and vanilla. Spread evenly over top of cheesecake. Spoon out 2 to 3 tablespoons of cherry sauce from pie filling; drop by teaspoonfuls onto Light Sour Cream topping. Carefully pull knife or spatula through cherry sauce, forming hearts. Cover; refrigerate 4 hours or overnight. To serve, in medium bowl stir together remaining pie filling and liqueur; spoon over cheesecake. Store refrigerated. **YIELD:** 12 servings.

Nutrition Information (1 serving): Calories 490; Protein 7g; Carbohydrate 48g; Fat 29g; Cholesterol 153mg; Sodium 310mg.

Double Chocolate Cheesecake With Raspberry Sauce

*Chocolate and white chocolate combine in this heavenly
cheesecake topped with raspberry sauce.*

Preparation time: 45 minutes • Baking time: 4 hours 25 minutes • Chilling time: 8 hours • (pictured)

Crust

1 1/3 cups graham cracker
   crumbs
1/4 cup
   LAND O LAKES® Butter,
   melted
2 tablespoons sugar

Filling

1 cup sugar
4 (8 ounce) packages cream
   cheese, softened
4 eggs
1 (12 ounce) package (2 cups)
   vanilla milk chips, melted*
1 cup chocolate fudge topping,
   warmed

Sauce

2 (10 ounce) packages frozen
   raspberries in syrup, thawed
1 tablespoon cornstarch

Heat oven to 325°. In small bowl stir together all crust ingredients.
Press crumb mixture evenly onto bottom of 9-inch springform pan.
Bake 10 minutes; cool. In large mixer bowl combine 1 cup sugar
and cream cheese. Beat at medium speed, scraping bowl often, until
light and fluffy (3 to 4 minutes). Continue beating, adding eggs one
at a time, until well mixed (1 to 2 minutes). Stir in melted vanilla
milk chips. (Mixture may look lumpy.) Pour half of cream cheese
mixture into prepared crust. Spoon 1/2 cup chocolate fudge topping
over cream cheese mixture in crust; swirl with knife. Top with
remaining cream cheese mixture. Spoon remaining chocolate fudge
topping over cream cheese mixture; swirl with knife. Bake for 65 to
75 minutes or until just set 2 inches from edge of pan. Turn off
oven; leave cheesecake in oven 2 hours.

Loosen sides of cheesecake from pan by running knife around
inside of pan. Cool completely. Cover; refrigerate 8 hours or
overnight. Meanwhile, press raspberries through strainer; discard
seeds. (Strain raspberries again, if seeds still remain.) In 1-quart
saucepan, with a wire whisk, stir together strained raspberries and
cornstarch. Cook over medium heat, stirring constantly, until
mixture comes to a full boil (4 to 8 minutes). Boil, stirring
constantly, until slightly thickened (2 minutes). Remove from
heat. Cool 5 minutes; stir. Cover; refrigerate until serving time.
To serve, spoon raspberry sauce over each slice of cheesecake.
Store refrigerated. **YIELD:** 12 servings.

*12 ounces white chocolate, chopped, can be substituted for 1 (12 ounce) package
  (2 cups) vanilla milk chips.

*Nutrition Information (1 serving): Calories 700; Protein 12g; Carbohydrate 68g; Fat 44g;
Cholesterol 165mg; Sodium 410mg.*

Chocolate Mocha Cheesecake

*Two favorite flavors, coffee and chocolate, are combined
in this rich and creamy cheesecake.*

Preparation time: 40 minutes • Baking time: 3 hours 20 minutes • Chilling time: 8 hours

Crust

1 1/3 cups graham cracker
   crumbs
1/4 cup
   LAND O LAKES® Butter,
   melted
2 tablespoons sugar

Filling

3/4 cup sugar
1/2 cup
   LAND O LAKES®
   Light Sour Cream
   or dairy sour cream
3 (8 ounce) packages cream
   cheese, softened
3 tablespoons all-purpose flour
3 eggs
1 tablespoon vanilla
1 to 2 teaspoons instant coffee
   granules
1 tablespoon warm water
1/4 cup sugar
1/4 cup unsweetened cocoa
3 tablespoons
   LAND O LAKES® Butter,
   melted

Topping

2 (1.4 ounce) English toffee
   bars, chopped

Heat oven to 325°. In medium bowl stir together all crust ingredients. Press crumb mixture evenly onto bottom of 9-inch springform pan. Bake 10 minutes; cool. In large mixer bowl combine 3/4 cup sugar, Light Sour Cream, cream cheese and flour. Beat at medium speed, scraping bowl often, until smooth and creamy (2 to 3 minutes). Add eggs and vanilla. Continue beating, scraping bowl often, until well mixed (1 to 2 minutes). In medium bowl stir together coffee granules and water until granules dissolve. Add 1 cup cream cheese mixture; stir until well mixed. Set aside. In small bowl combine all remaining filling ingredients; stir until smooth. Add cocoa mixture to remaining cream cheese mixture; by hand, stir until well mixed. Pour chocolate cream cheese mixture into crust. Pour coffee mixture over chocolate mixture. Pull knife through batter for marbled effect. Bake for 50 to 70 minutes or until center is set. Turn off oven; leave cheesecake in oven for 2 hours. Loosen sides of cheesecake from pan by running knife around inside of pan. Sprinkle topping over cheesecake. Cool completely. Cover; refrigerate 8 hours or overnight. Store refrigerated. **YIELD:** 12 servings.

Nutrition Information (1 serving): Calories 440; Protein 8g; Carbohydrate 35g; Fat 32g; Cholesterol 136mg; Sodium 360mg.

Strawberry Rhubarb Ribboned Cheesecake

Strawberry and rhubarb filling makes this
cheesecake extra-special.

Preparation time: 45 minutes • Baking time: 3 hours 15 minutes • Chilling time: 8 hours

Crust
1 cup all-purpose flour
1/4 cup sugar
1/3 cup
  LAND O LAKES® Butter,
  cut into 1-inch pieces
2 tablespoons milk

Ribbon Filling
1/3 cup sugar
1/4 cup cornstarch
1 cup fresh or frozen
  strawberries
1 cup fresh or frozen rhubarb,
  cut into 1-inch pieces
1/3 cup water

Cheesecake
5 (8 ounce) packages cream
  cheese, softened
3 eggs
1 1/4 cups sugar
3 tablespoons all-purpose flour
1 tablespoon grated lemon peel

Heat oven to 400°. In small bowl stir together 1 cup flour and 1/4 cup sugar. Cut butter into flour mixture until mixture forms coarse crumbs; stir in milk to moisten. Press crust mixture on bottom and 1 inch up sides of 9 or 10-inch springform pan. Bake for 8 to 10 minutes or until light golden brown; remove from oven. Reduce heat to 375°. Meanwhile, in 2-quart saucepan combine 1/3 cup sugar and cornstarch. Stir in all remaining ribbon filling ingredients. Cook over medium heat, stirring constantly, until mixture comes to a full boil (5 to 7 minutes). Boil, stirring constantly, until thickened (1 minute); remove from heat.

In large mixer bowl beat cream cheese at high speed until light and fluffy (2 to 3 minutes). Continue beating, adding eggs 1 at a time, and scraping bowl often, until well mixed. Reduce speed to low. Add all remaining ingredients; continue beating scraping bowl often, until well mixed. Spoon half of cheesecake mixture over cooled crust. Dollop half of ribbon filling over cheesecake mixture; swirl with knife. Top with remaining cheesecake mixture. Dollop remaining ribbon filling over cheesecake; swirl with knife. Bake for 60 to 75 minutes or until center is just set. If browning too quickly, loosely cover with aluminum foil. Turn off oven; leave cheesecake in oven for 2 hours. Loosen sides of cheesecake from pan by running knife around inside of pan. Cool completely. Cover; refrigerate 8 hours or overnight. Store refrigerated. **YIELD:** 16 servings.

Nutrition Information (1 serving): Calories 430; Protein 8g; Carbohydrate 35g; Fat 30g;
Cholesterol 130mg; Sodium 260mg.

Cool Key Lime Cheesecake

A cheesecake version of a favorite
Florida dessert.

Preparation time: 30 minutes • Chilling time: 4 hours 45 minutes • (pictured)

Crust

1 cup graham cracker crumbs
1/4 cup sugar
1/3 cup
   LAND O LAKES® Butter,
   melted

Filling

1 cup lime juice
1/4 cup water
2 (1/4 ounce) envelopes
   unflavored gelatin
1 1/2 cups sugar
5 eggs, slightly beaten
1 tablespoon grated lime peel
1/2 cup
   LAND O LAKES® Butter,
   softened
2 (8 ounce) packages cream
   cheese, softened
1/2 cup whipping cream

Sweetened whipped cream
Lime slices

In medium bowl stir together all crust ingredients. Press on bottom of 9-inch springform pan; set aside. In 2-quart saucepan combine lime juice, water and gelatin. Let stand 5 minutes to soften. Add sugar, eggs and lime peel. Cook over medium heat, stirring constantly, until mixture just comes to a boil (7 to 8 minutes). DO NOT BOIL. Set aside. In large mixer bowl combine butter and cream cheese. Beat at medium speed, scraping bowl often, until well mixed (1 to 2 minutes). Continue beating, gradually adding hot lime mixture, until well mixed (1 to 2 minutes). Refrigerate, stirring occasionally, until cool (about 45 minutes). In chilled small mixer bowl beat chilled whipping cream at high speed, scraping bowl often, until stiff peaks form (1 to 2 minutes). Fold into lime mixture. Pour into prepared crust. Cover; refrigerate until firm (3 to 4 hours). Loosen sides of cheesecake from pan by running knife around inside of pan; remove pan. Garnish top of cheesecake with sweetened whipped cream. If desired, garnish with lime slices. **YIELD:** 12 servings.

Nutrition Information (1 serving): Calories 460; Protein 7g; Carbohydrate 37g; Fat 33g; Cholesterol 179mg; Sodium 325mg.

Easy Mini-Cheesecakes

Making cheesecake has never been so easy!

Preparation time: 30 minutes • Baking time: 40 minutes • Chilling time: 2 hours • (pictured)

12 foil cupcake liners

12 vanilla wafer cookies
1/2 cup sugar
2 (8 ounce) packages cream
   cheese, softened
2 eggs
1 teaspoon vanilla
1 (8 ounce) carton (1 cup)
   LAND O LAKES®
   Light Sour Cream
   <u>or</u> dairy sour cream
2 tablespoons sugar
1 teaspoon vanilla

Chocolate curls
Cut-up fruit
Powdered sugar

Heat oven to 325°. Line 12-cup muffin pan with foil liners; place one cookie in each liner. In large mixer bowl combine 1/2 cup sugar, cream cheese, eggs and vanilla. Beat at medium speed, scraping bowl often, until smooth (2 to 3 minutes). Pour over each cookie, filling cup 3/4 full. Bake for 30 minutes. Meanwhile, in small bowl stir together Light Sour Cream, 2 tablespoons sugar and vanilla. Spoon about 1 tablespoon Light Sour Cream mixture onto each hot cheesecake. Continue baking for 8 to 10 minutes or until set. Cool; remove from pan. Cover; refrigerate until firm (1 to 2 hours). Store refrigerated. To serve, garnish with chocolate curls, fruit and powdered sugar. **YIELD:** 12 servings.

Nutrition Information (1 serving): Calories 250; Protein 5g; Carbohydrate 20g; Fat 17g; Cholesterol 83mg; Sodium 150mg.

Tarts
& Pies

*There is nothing
prettier than an
elegant tart
to serve when
company's coming.
And who can resist
a slice of
homemade pie?
Try both our
bake-ahead
and
no-bake versions!*

Strawberries N' Cream Tart, page 50

Strawberries N' Cream Tart

Luscious ripe berries sit in
a delightful, fluffy cream.

Preparation time: 45 minutes • Baking time: 15 minutes • Cooling time: 30 minutes •Chilling time: 1 hour • (pictured on page 48)

Crust
1/2 cup
  LAND O LAKES® Butter,
  softened
1/3 cup sugar
1 1/4 cups all-purpose flour
2 tablespoons milk
1/2 teaspoon almond extract

Filling
1 (3 ounce) package cream
  cheese, softened
1/2 cup powdered sugar
1/2 teaspoon almond extract
1 cup whipping cream

Topping
1 pint fresh strawberries,
  sliced, <u>or</u> fresh raspberries
2 to 4 tablespoons strawberry
  <u>or</u> raspberry jelly, melted

Heat oven to 400°. In small mixer bowl beat butter and sugar at medium speed, scraping bowl often, until light and fluffy (1 to 2 minutes). Add flour, milk and 1/2 teaspoon almond extract. Reduce speed to low; continue beating, scraping bowl often, until mixture leaves sides of bowl and forms a ball. Press dough onto bottom and up sides of greased 10-inch tart pan or 12-inch pizza pan; prick with fork. Bake for 10 to 15 minutes or until light golden brown. Cool. In small mixer bowl combine cream cheese, powdered sugar and 1/2 teaspoon almond extract. Beat at medium speed, scraping bowl often, until light and fluffy (1 to 2 minutes). Continue beating, gradually adding whipping cream, until mixture is thick and fluffy (2 to 3 minutes). Spread over top of cooled crust. Refrigerate at least 1 hour. Just before serving, arrange fruit on filling. Brush or drizzle melted jelly over fruit. **YIELD:** 10 servings.

Nutrition Information (1 serving): Calories 320; Protein 3g; Carbohydrate 29g; Fat 22g; Cholesterol 68mg; Sodium 133mg.

Bavarian Apple Tart

*Moist, sweet apples are nestled in a cream cheese
layer atop a sweet crust.*

Preparation time: 45 minutes • Baking time: 55 minutes

Crust
1 cup all-purpose flour
1/3 cup sugar
1/2 cup
   LAND O LAKES® Butter,
   softened
1/4 teaspoon vanilla

Filling
1/2 cup sugar
2 (8 ounce) packages cream
   cheese, softened
2 eggs
1 teaspoon vanilla

4 cups (4 medium) peeled,
   sliced 1/4-inch tart
   cooking apples
1/3 cup sugar
1/2 teaspoon cinnamon
1/2 teaspoon nutmeg
Dash cardamom

1/4 cup sliced almonds

Sweetened whipped cream

Heat oven to 375°. In small mixer bowl combine flour, 1/3 cup sugar, butter and 1/4 teaspoon vanilla. Beat at medium speed, scraping bowl often, until dough leaves sides of bowl and forms a ball (2 to 3 minutes). With lightly floured hands, press on bottom of 10-inch springform pan. In same small mixer bowl combine 1/2 cup sugar, cream cheese, eggs and 1 teaspoon vanilla. Beat at medium speed, scraping bowl often, until smooth (2 to 3 minutes). Spread over crust. In large bowl place apples. Sprinkle with 1/3 cup sugar, cinnamon, nutmeg and cardamom; toss to coat. Arrange apples over filling. Bake for 35 to 45 minutes or until apples are fork-tender. Sprinkle with almonds; continue baking for 5 to 10 minutes or until almonds are lightly browned. Cool completely. Remove rim from springform pan. Cut into wedges; serve with whipped cream.
YIELD: 12 servings.

Nutrition Information (1 serving): Calories 360; Protein 6g; Carbohydrate 34g; Fat 23g; Cholesterol 108mg; Sodium 202mg.

Pear Custard Tart

*A velvety custard bakes around slices of red,
blushed pears in a flaky pastry tart.*

Preparation time: 1 hour • Baking time: 51 minutes • (pictured)

Pastry

1 2/3 cups all-purpose flour
2 tablespoons sugar
3/4 cup
   LAND O LAKES® Butter
1 egg, slightly beaten
1 tablespoon milk

Filling

3/4 cup sugar
2 tablespoons cornstarch
2 cups milk
5 egg yolks, slightly beaten
2 tablespoons
   LAND O LAKES® Butter
2 teaspoons vanilla
1 tablespoon lemon juice
3 medium ripe red pears, sliced
   1/4-inch

Powdered sugar

Heat oven to 400°. In large bowl stir together flour and 2 tablespoons sugar. Cut in 3/4 cup butter until crumbly. With fork mix in egg and 1 tablespoon milk just until moistened. Shape into ball; on lightly floured surface roll into 14-inch circle. Place in 10-inch tart pan; press on bottom and up sides of pan. Cut away excess pastry. Prick with fork generously. Bake for 9 to 11 minutes or until lightly browned. <u>Reduce oven to 375°.</u> Meanwhile, in 2-quart saucepan combine 3/4 cup sugar and cornstarch. Gradually stir in 2 cups milk. Cook over medium heat, stirring constantly, until mixture is thickened and comes to a full boil (10 to 15 minutes). Boil, stirring constantly, 1 minute.

Place egg yolks in medium bowl; slowly whisk <u>2/3</u> of hot milk mixture into egg yolks. Return to same pan with remaining hot milk mixture. Continue cooking, stirring constantly, until mixture comes to a full boil (3 to 5 minutes). Boil, stirring constantly, 1 minute. Remove from heat; stir in 2 tablespoons butter and vanilla until butter is melted. Place lemon juice in small bowl; dip pear slices into lemon juice. Pour custard into baked pastry; arrange pear slices in custard. Bake for 30 to 40 minutes or until custard is set. Cool 1 hour before serving. Sprinkle with powdered sugar. **YIELD:** 8 servings.

Nutrition Information (1 serving): Calories 490; Protein 8g; Carbohydrate 56g; Fat 27g; Cholesterol 260mg; Sodium 250mg.

Stars & Stripes Tart

*A rich fruit tart in celebration
of our patriotism.*

Preparation time: 45 minutes • Baking time: 18 minutes • Cooling time: 30 minutes • Chilling time: 1 hour • (pictured)

Crust

1 cup
   LAND O LAKES® Butter,
   softened
1/2 cup sugar
2 1/2 cups all-purpose flour
1/3 cup milk

Filling

3 (3 ounce) packages cream
   cheese, softened
3/4 cup powdered sugar
1 teaspoon grated orange peel
1 tablespoon orange juice

Topping

1 pint strawberries, hulled,
   sliced <u>or</u> raspberries*
1 cup fresh blueberries*
1/4 cup apple jelly, melted

Heat oven to 400°. In large mixer bowl combine butter and sugar. Beat at medium speed, scraping bowl often, until light and fluffy (1 to 2 minutes). Add flour and milk; beat at low speed until well mixed. Press dough on bottom and 1/2 inch up sides of 13x9-inch baking pan. Prick bottom with fork. Bake for 14 to 18 minutes or until lightly browned. Cool. In small mixer bowl combine all filling ingredients; beat at medium speed, scraping bowl often, until light and fluffy (1 to 2 minutes). Spread over top of cooled crust. Refrigerate 1 hour or until firm. Just before serving, arrange fruit on filling in design of American flag, using strawberry slices for stripes and blueberries for stars. Brush fruit and filling with melted apple jelly. **YIELD:** 12 servings.

*4 cups of your favorite fruit (kiwi, mandarin orange segments, pineapple, etc.), arranged in any design, can be substituted for strawberries and blueberries.

Nutrition Information (1 serving): Calories 350; Protein 4g; Carbohydrate 44g; Fat 18g; Cholesterol 50mg; Sodium 184mg.

Crisp Phyllo Petals With Berries

The pastry of this luscious pie is made from phyllo dough, the filling from sweetened whipped cream and summer's berries.

Preparation time: 1 hour 15 minutes • Baking time: 12 minutes • (pictured)

Crust

6 sheets frozen phyllo dough, thawed

1/4 cup
  LAND O LAKES® Butter, melted

2 tablespoons powdered sugar

Filling

1 cup whipping cream

1/4 cup powdered sugar

2 tablespoons orange juice

1/2 teaspoon vanilla

4 cups (1 quart) fresh strawberries, hulled, sliced 1/4-inch

1 cup fresh raspberries

1 cup fresh blueberries

Powdered sugar

Heat oven to 400°. Lay one sheet of phyllo over 9-inch pie pan, gently gathering to form ruffled and uneven rim. Fit into pan, allowing ends to hang over. (Keep remaining phyllo sheets covered while assembling crust.) Brush phyllo with about <u>2 teaspoons</u> melted butter; sprinkle with about <u>1 teaspoon</u> powdered sugar. Fit second sheet of phyllo in pan at right angles to first. Brush with <u>2 teaspoons</u> butter; sprinkle with <u>1 teaspoon</u> powdered sugar. Repeat layering, buttering and sugaring with remaining phyllo sheets, butter and powdered sugar. Bake for 7 to 12 minutes or until golden brown. Let stand 5 minutes; remove from pan. Place on serving plate. Sprinkle powdered sugar over crust.

Just before serving, in chilled small mixer bowl beat chilled whipping cream at high speed, scraping bowl often, until soft peaks form (1 to 2 minutes). Continue beating, gradually adding 1/4 cup powdered sugar, until stiff peaks form (1 to 2 minutes). Fold in orange juice and vanilla. Fold in <u>2 cups</u> strawberries, <u>1/2 cup</u> raspberries and <u>1/2 cup</u> blueberries. Spoon whipped cream mixture into center of crust. Arrange remaining berries on top of whipped cream mixture; sprinkle with powdered sugar. **YIELD:** 6 servings.

Nutrition Information (1 serving): Calories 310; Protein 3g; Carbohydrate 26g; Fat 23g; Cholesterol 75mg; Sodium 151mg.

Chocolate Peanut Butter Tart

*The name alone describes this rich dessert that can be
served as a tart or a bar.*

Preparation time: 1 hour • Chilling time: 2 hours • (pictured)

Crust
1 1/2 cups graham cracker
  crumbs
1/3 cup unsalted peanuts,
  chopped
1/2 cup LAND O LAKES®
  Butter, melted

Fudge Layer
2 tablespoons
  LAND O LAKES® Butter
1 cup semi-sweet real chocolate
  chips
1 tablespoon water
1/4 cup powdered sugar

Filling
1/3 cup powdered sugar
1/2 cup creamy peanut butter
1/4 cup
  LAND O LAKES® Butter,
  softened
1 (3 ounce) package cream
  cheese, softened

Chocolate Drizzle
1 tablespoon
  LAND O LAKES® Butter
2 tablespoons semi-sweet real
  chocolate chips

In medium bowl stir together all crust ingredients. Press crust mixture evenly on bottom of 10-inch tart pan or pizza pan; refrigerate until firm (5 to 10 minutes). In 1-quart saucepan combine 2 tablespoons butter, 1 cup chocolate chips and water. Cook over medium heat, stirring occasionally, until melted (3 to 5 minutes). Remove from heat; stir in 1/4 cup powdered sugar until smooth. Spread fudge mixture over crust; set aside. In medium mixer bowl combine all filling ingredients. Beat at high speed, scraping bowl often, until light and fluffy (2 to 3 minutes). Spread peanut butter mixture over fudge layer. In 1-quart saucepan combine 1 tablespoon butter and 2 tablespoons chocolate chips. Cook over low heat, stirring constantly, until melted and smooth (2 to 3 minutes). Drizzle over filling. Cover; refrigerate at least 2 hours. **YIELD:** 16 servings.

VARIATION

Chocolate Peanut Butter Bars: Prepare recipe as directed above, using a 13x9-inch pan in place of 10-inch tart pan or pizza pan. **YIELD:** 32 bars.

Nutrition Information (1 serving): Calories 280; Protein 4g; Carbohydrate 19g; Fat 23g; Cholesterol 35mg; Sodium 220mg.

Espresso Ice Cream Pie

*Chocolate and coffee team up in
this frozen dessert.*

Preparation time: 30 minutes • Freezing time: 1 hour

Crust
1 1/2 cups (about 30) crushed
   chocolate wafer cookies
1/4 cup sugar
1/4 cup
   LAND O LAKES® Butter,
   melted

Filling
1/2 cup chocolate fudge
   topping
1 tablespoon instant espresso
   coffee granules <u>or</u> instant
   coffee granules
3 tablespoons dark corn syrup
1 teaspoon water

1 quart (4 cups) French vanilla
   ice cream, slightly softened

Topping
Sweetened whipped cream
Chocolate curls
Grated orange <u>or</u> lemon peel

In medium bowl stir together all crust ingredients. Press crust mixture on bottom and sides of 9-inch pie pan. Spread fudge topping onto cookie crust. (If fudge topping is too thick to spread, warm to desired spreading consistency.) In small bowl stir together espresso granules, corn syrup and water; set aside. Carefully spoon half of ice cream into pie crust, pressing to fill bottom of pie. Swirl half of espresso mixture gently through ice cream in crust. Spoon remaining ice cream into pie; decoratively swirl remaining espresso mixture through ice cream. Freeze at least 1 hour or until firm. Serve pie with sweetened whipped cream, chocolate curls and grated orange peel. **YIELD:** 8 servings.

Nutrition Information (1 serving): Calories 390; Protein 5g; Carbohydrate 54g; Fat 19g; Cholesterol 55mg; Sodium 180mg.

Ice Cream Lemonade Pie

*This pie can't be beat when you want
a cool, refreshing dessert.*

Preparation time: 45 minutes • Baking time: 15 minutes • Chilling time: 1 hour • Freezing time: 8 hours

Crust

1 1/4 cups finely crushed
   pretzels
3 tablespoons sugar
6 tablespoons
   LAND O LAKES® Butter,
   melted

Filling

1/4 cup
   LAND O LAKES® Butter
1/3 cup sugar
3 egg yolks, slightly beaten,
   <u>reserve whites</u>
1 tablespoon lemon juice

1 quart (4 cups) vanilla ice
   cream, slightly softened
1 (6 ounce) can frozen
   lemonade concentrate,
   thawed

Meringue

3 reserved egg whites
3 tablespoons sugar
1/8 teaspoon cream of tartar

Heat oven to 350°. In medium bowl stir together all crust ingredients. Press on bottom and sides of 9-inch pie pan. Bake for 10 minutes; cool completely. In 2-quart saucepan melt 1/4 cup butter. In small bowl stir together 1/3 cup sugar and egg yolks. Gradually stir sugar mixture into melted butter. Cook over medium heat, stirring constantly, until slightly thickened (2 to 4 minutes). Stir in lemon juice. Refrigerate 1 hour. In large bowl stir together ice cream and lemonade concentrate until well blended. Spread <u>2 cups</u> ice cream mixture on prepared crust. Cover; freeze 1 hour.

Cover remaining ice cream mixture; freeze until ready to spread. Spread cooled filling over ice cream; carefully spread remaining ice cream mixture over filling. Freeze at least 1 hour. <u>Heat oven to 425°.</u> In small mixer bowl beat egg whites on high speed, scraping bowl often, until soft peaks form (1 to 2 minutes). Reduce speed to medium. Continue beating, scraping bowl often and gradually adding sugar and cream of tartar, until stiff peaks form (1 to 2 minutes). Spread carefully onto frozen pie, sealing edges of crust. Bake for 3 to 5 minutes or until lightly browned. Freeze until firm (6 hours or overnight). **YIELD:** 8 servings.

Nutrition Information (1 serving): Calories 440; Protein 6g; Carbohydrate 54g; Fat 24g; Cholesterol 150mg; Sodium 380mg.

Choco-Peanut Butter Ice Cream Pie

*Chocolate and peanut butter are mounded high
in this frozen ice cream pie.*

Preparation time: 30 minutes • Baking time: 8 minutes • Cooling time: 15 minutes • Freezing time: 6 hours • (pictured)

Crust

1 1/2 cups graham cracker
    crumbs
3 tablespoons sugar
2 tablespoons chopped salted
    peanuts
1/4 cup
    LAND O LAKES® Butter,
    melted

Filling

2 cups chocolate ice cream,
    softened slightly
1 quart (4 cups) vanilla ice
    cream, slightly softened
1/3 cup peanut butter
2 tablespoons chopped salted
    peanuts

Chocolate syrup

Heat oven to 350°. In small bowl stir together all crust ingredients. Press on bottom and up sides of 9-inch or 10-inch pie pan. Bake for 6 to 8 minutes or until lightly browned. Cool completely. Spread softened chocolate ice cream over bottom of cooled pie crust. Freeze until firm (about 30 minutes). In large mixer bowl combine vanilla ice cream and peanut butter. Beat at low speed, scraping bowl often, until peanut butter is evenly distributed. Freeze until ice cream and peanut butter mixture holds soft mounds (30 to 45 minutes). Spoon ice cream and peanut butter mixture over chocolate ice cream layer. Spread to edges of crust, mounding slightly higher in center. Sprinkle with 2 tablespoons chopped peanuts. Freeze 4 to 5 hours or until firm. Let stand at room temperature 5 minutes before serving; drizzle with chocolate syrup. **YIELD:** 8 servings.

TIP: Do not use 8-inch pie pan.

Nutrition Information (1 serving): Calories 420; Protein 9g; Carbohydrate 43g; Fat 26g; Cholesterol 61mg; Sodium 325mg.

Cherry Orchard Pie

Grated orange peel spices this eye-catching lattice-top cherry pie.

Preparation time: 45 minutes • Baking time: 1 hour • (pictured)

Crust

2 cups all-purpose flour

1/4 teaspoon salt

2/3 cup
  LAND O LAKES® Butter or
  shortening

4 to 5 tablespoons cold water

Filling

1 cup sugar

1/3 cup all-purpose flour

1/8 teaspoon salt

2 (16 ounce) cans red tart
  pitted cherries, drained

1 teaspoon grated orange peel

Milk
Sugar

Heat oven to 400°. In large bowl stir together 2 cups flour and 1/4 teaspoon salt. Cut in butter until crumbly. With fork mix in water until flour is moistened. Divide pastry in half; shape each half into a ball. On lightly floured surface roll 1 pastry ball into 12-inch circle. Place in 9-inch pie pan. Trim pastry to 1/2 inch from rim of pan; set aside. In large bowl combine sugar, 1/3 cup flour and 1/8 teaspoon salt. Add cherries and orange peel; toss lightly to coat. Spoon into prepared crust. With remaining half of pastry prepare lattice top. Roll pastry into 11-inch circle. With sharp knife or pastry wheel, cut circle into 10 (1/2-inch) strips. Place 5 strips, 1 inch apart, across filling in pie pan. Place remaining 5 strips, 1 inch apart, at right angles to the strips already in place. With kitchen shears, trim strips. Fold trimmed edge of bottom pastry over strips; build up an edge. Seal; crimp or flute edge. Brush strips with milk; sprinkle with sugar. Cover edge of crust with 2-inch strip of aluminum foil. Bake for 50 to 60 minutes or until crust is golden brown and filling bubbles in center. If desired, remove aluminum foil during last 5 minutes. If browning too quickly, shield lattice strips with aluminum foil. **YIELD:** 8 servings.

Nutrition Information (1 serving): Calories 420; Protein 5g; Carbohydrate 68g; Fat 16g; Cholesterol 41mg; Sodium 260mg.

Crumb Top Rhubarb Pie

Pecans and a crumb topping crown
this delicious country favorite.

Preparation time: 30 minutes • Baking time: 1 hour

Crust

1 cup all-purpose flour
1/8 teaspoon salt
1/3 cup
   LAND O LAKES® Butter <u>or</u>
   shortening
3 to 4 tablespoons cold water

Filling

1 1/4 cups sugar
3 tablespoons cornstarch
1/2 teaspoon cinnamon
1/4 teaspoon nutmeg
4 cups sliced 1/4-inch fresh
   rhubarb

2/3 cup chopped pecans

Topping

1 cup all-purpose flour
2/3 cup sugar
1/2 cup
   LAND O LAKES® Butter

Heat oven to 400°. In large bowl stir together 1 cup flour and salt. Cut in 1/3 cup butter until crumbly. With fork mix in water until flour is moistened. Shape into a ball. On lightly floured surface roll pastry ball into 12-inch circle. Place in 9-inch deep dish pie pan. Crimp or flute crust; set aside. In large bowl stir together all filling ingredients <u>except</u> rhubarb and pecans. Stir in rhubarb until well coated with sugar mixture. Spoon into prepared crust. Sprinkle with pecans; set aside. In medium bowl stir together 1 cup flour and 2/3 cup sugar. Cut in butter until crumbly. Sprinkle mixture over rhubarb. Cover edge of crust with 2-inch strip of aluminum foil. Bake for 50 to 60 minutes or until topping is golden brown and filling bubbles around edges. If desired, remove aluminum foil during last 10 minutes. **YIELD:** 8 servings.

Nutrition Information (1 serving): Calories 560; Protein 5g; Carbohydrate 79g; Fat 26g; Cholesterol 52mg; Sodium 230mg.

Blueberry Sour Cream Pie

*An easy cream pie turns elegant when topped with
fresh blueberries.*

Preparation time: 15 minutes • Baking time: 12 minutes • Cooling time: 30 minutes • Chilling time: 2 hours

Crust
1 1/2 cups graham cracker
   crumbs
1/3 cup
   LAND O LAKES® Butter,
   melted

Filling
1 (8 ounce) carton (1 cup)
   LAND O LAKES®
   Light Sour Cream
   <u>or</u> dairy sour cream
1 1/4 cups milk
1 (3 1/2 ounce) package vanilla
   instant pudding and
   pie filling*
1 cup fresh blueberries <u>or</u>
   favorite fresh fruit

Heat oven to 350°. In medium bowl stir together graham cracker crumbs and butter. Press on bottom and sides of 9-inch pie pan. Bake for 10 to 12 minutes or until lightly browned; cool completely. In small mixer bowl place Light Sour Cream; beat at medium speed, gradually adding milk, until smooth (1 to 2 minutes). Continue beating, gradually adding pudding and scraping bowl often, until well mixed and thickened (1 to 2 minutes). Pour into crust. Refrigerate until set (1 to 2 hours). Garnish with blueberries. **YIELD:** 8 servings.

*1 (0.9 ounce) package vanilla sugar-free instant pudding and pie filling can be substituted for 1 (3 1/2 ounce) package vanilla instant pudding and pie filling.

*Nutrition Information (1 serving): Calories 240; Protein 4g; Carbohydrate 32g; Fat 11g;
Cholesterol 28mg; Sodium 420mg.*

Creamy Banana Pie With Lemon Zest

*This heavenly banana cream pie is
both light and luscious.*

Preparation time: 1 hour • Baking time: 10 minutes • Cooling time: 30 minutes • Chilling time: 7 hours • (pictured)

Crust

1 cup all-purpose flour

1/8 teaspoon salt

1/3 cup
   LAND O LAKES® Butter
   or shortening

3 to 4 tablespoons cold water

Filling

3/4 cup sugar

1/4 cup cornstarch

1 (1/4 ounce) envelope
   unflavored gelatin

2 1/2 cups milk

4 egg yolks, slightly beaten

2 tablespoons
   LAND O LAKES® Butter

1 tablespoon vanilla

2 teaspoons grated lemon peel

2 tablespoons lemon juice

3 medium bananas, sliced
   1/4-inch

3/4 cup whipping cream

Topping

1/4 cup apple jelly

1 tablespoon lemon juice

1 medium banana, sliced
   1/4-inch

Heat oven to 475°. In large bowl stir together flour and salt. Cut in 1/3 cup butter until crumbly. With fork mix in water until flour is moistened. Shape into a ball. On lightly floured surface roll pastry ball into 12-inch circle. Place in 9-inch pie pan. Crimp or flute crust. With fork prick bottom and sides of pastry. Bake for 8 to 10 minutes or until lightly browned; cool completely. Meanwhile, in 2-quart saucepan combine sugar, cornstarch and gelatin. Gradually stir in milk and egg yolks. Cook over medium heat, stirring constantly, until mixture comes to a full boil (10 to 12 minutes). Stir in 2 tablespoons butter, vanilla and lemon peel until butter is melted; pour filling into large bowl. Cover; refrigerate until thickened (about 2 hours). Place 2 tablespoons lemon juice in small bowl; dip 3 sliced bananas into lemon juice. In chilled small mixer bowl beat chilled whipping cream, scraping bowl often, until stiff peaks form (1 to 2 minutes). By hand, fold whipped cream and bananas into pudding mixture. Pour into baked pie shell. Refrigerate at least 5 hours or until firm. Just before serving, in 1-quart saucepan stir together apple jelly and 1 tablespoon lemon juice. Cook over low heat, stirring occasionally, until apple jelly is melted (3 to 4 minutes). Arrange remaining banana slices 1 inch from outside edge of pie to form a circle. Spoon or drizzle apple jelly mixture over bananas. **YIELD:** 8 servings.

Nutrition Information (1 serving): Calories 470; Protein 8g; Carbohydrate 60g; Fat 23g; Cholesterol 174mg; Sodium 200mg.

Mixed Berry Meringue Pie

*Meringue forms the crust of this fresh
berry pie.*

Preparation time: 1 hour • Baking time: 1 hour 45 minutes • Cooling time: 1 hour • Chilling time: 2 hours • (pictured)

Meringue
2 egg whites
1/4 teaspoon cream of tartar
1/2 cup sugar

Filling
3/4 cup powdered sugar
1 (8 ounce) carton (1 cup)
   LAND O LAKES®
   Light Sour Cream
   or dairy sour cream
4 ounces cream cheese
1 tablespoon orange juice
1 teaspoon grated orange peel

Topping
1 pint fresh strawberries,
   cleaned, hulled
1 cup fresh raspberries*
1/4 cup apple jelly, melted

Heat oven to 275°. In small mixer bowl combine egg whites and cream of tartar. Beat at high speed until foamy. Continue beating, gradually adding sugar and scraping bowl often, until glossy and stiff peaks form (3 to 4 minutes). Spoon into well greased (bottom only) 9-inch pie pan; using back of spoon, spread meringue over bottom and up sides. Bake for 1 hour. Turn off oven; leave meringue in oven with door closed for 45 minutes. Finish meringue cooling at room temperature. In small mixer bowl combine all filling ingredients. Beat at medium speed, scraping bowl often, until smooth and creamy (2 to 3 minutes). Spoon filling into meringue shell; using back of spoon spread over bottom and up sides. Refrigerate 2 hours or until firm. Just before serving, place strawberries, stem side down, on filling. Sprinkle raspberries over strawberries. Brush or drizzle melted apple jelly over berries. **YIELD:** 10 servings.

* 1 cup blueberries or combination of raspberries and blueberries can be substituted for 1 cup raspberries.

TIP: Meringue can be prepared day before serving.

Nutrition Information (1 serving): Calories 180; Protein 4g; Carbohydrate 30g; Fat 6g; Cholesterol 16mg; Sodium 73mg.

Blue Ribbon Apple Pie

Pour whipping cream into this delectable apple pie; the cream thickens and settles around juicy apples.

Preparation time: 1 hour • Baking time: 1 hour • Cooling time: 30 minutes • (pictured)

Crust

2 cups all-purpose flour

1 teaspoon sugar

1/4 teaspoon salt

1/4 teaspoon cinnamon

1/4 teaspoon nutmeg

1/3 cup
LAND O LAKES® Butter

1/3 cup shortening

4 to 5 tablespoons cold water

Filling

1/2 cup sugar

1/4 cup firmly packed brown
sugar

1/4 cup all-purpose flour

1/2 teaspoon cinnamon

1/2 teaspoon nutmeg

6 cups (6 medium) peeled,
cored, sliced 1/4-inch tart
cooking apples

1 tablespoon
LAND O LAKES® Butter

1 teaspoon sugar

1/2 cup whipping cream

Heat oven to 400°. In large bowl stir together 2 cups flour, 1 teaspoon sugar, salt, 1/4 teaspoon cinnamon and 1/4 teaspoon nutmeg. Cut in 1/3 cup butter and shortening until crumbly. With fork mix in water until flour is moistened. Divide dough in half; shape into 2 balls and flatten. Wrap 1 ball in plastic food wrap; refrigerate. On lightly floured surface roll out other ball into 12-inch circle. Place in 9-inch pie pan. Trim pastry to 1/2-inch from rim of pan; set aside.

In large bowl combine all filling ingredients <u>except</u> apples, 1 tablespoon butter, 1 teaspoon sugar and whipping cream. Add apples; toss lightly to coat. Spoon into prepared crust. Roll remaining pastry ball into 12-inch circle; cut 8 large slits in top crust. Place over pie; crimp or flute crust. Brush with melted 1 tablespoon butter; sprinkle with 1 teaspoon sugar. Cover edge of crust with 2-inch strip of aluminum foil. Bake for 35 minutes; remove aluminum foil. Continue baking for 10 to 20 minutes or until crust is lightly browned and juice begins to bubble through slits in crust. Remove from oven; run knife through slits to open. Pour whipping cream evenly through all slits. Return to oven for 5 minutes to warm whipping cream. Cool pie 30 minutes; serve warm. **YIELD:** 8 servings.

TIP: If desired, omit whipping cream for a traditional apple pie.

Nutrition Information (1 serving): Calories 460; Protein 4g; Carbohydrate 60g; Fat 24g; Cholesterol 45mg; Sodium 170mg.

Pumpkin Squares

*An easy way to serve pumpkin pie
to a crowd.*

Preparation time: 30 minutes • Baking time: 1 hour • (pictured)

Crust
1 cup all-purpose flour
1/2 cup old-fashioned
   rolled oats
1/2 cup firmly packed
   brown sugar
1/2 cup
   LAND O LAKES® Butter,
   softened

Filling
3/4 cup sugar
1 (16 ounce) can pumpkin
1 (12 ounce) can evaporated
   milk
2 eggs
1 teaspoon cinnamon
1/2 teaspoon salt
1/2 teaspoon ginger
1/4 teaspoon cloves

Topping
1/2 cup firmly packed
   brown sugar
1/2 cup chopped pecans

Sweetened whipped cream

Heat oven to 350°. In small mixer bowl combine all crust ingredients. Beat at low speed, scraping bowl often, until crumbly (1 to 2 minutes). Press on bottom of 13x9-inch baking pan. Bake for 15 minutes. Meanwhile, in large mixer bowl combine all filling ingredients. Beat at medium speed, scraping bowl often, until smooth (1 to 2 minutes). Pour over crust; continue baking for 20 minutes. In small bowl stir together 1/2 cup brown sugar and pecans; sprinkle over filling. Continue baking for 15 to 25 minutes or until filling is firm to the touch or knife inserted in center comes out clean. Cool completely; cut into squares. Store refrigerated. **YIELD:** 12 servings.

Nutrition Information (1 serving): Calories 360; Protein 6g; Carbohydrate 49g; Fat 17g; Cholesterol 76mg; Sodium 220mg.

German Chocolate Cheesecake Pie

*A coconut almond crust is topped with a
chocolate cheesecake filling.*

Preparation time: 30 minutes • Baking time: 35 minutes • Chilling time: 2 hours

Crust
1 cup chopped toasted
   slivered almonds
1 cup flaked coconut
1/3 cup sugar
1/3 cup
   LAND O LAKES® Butter,
   melted

Filling
1/2 cup sugar
2 (8 ounce) packages
   cream cheese, softened
2 eggs
1 (4 ounce) bar sweet cooking
   chocolate, melted

Heat oven to 350°. In medium bowl stir together all crust ingredients; reserve 1/3 cup for topping. Press remaining crust mixture on bottom and halfway up sides of 9-inch pie pan. In large mixer bowl combine 1/2 cup sugar and cream cheese. Beat at medium speed, scraping bowl often, until light and fluffy (1 to 2 minutes). Add eggs; continue beating, scraping bowl often, until well mixed (1 to 2 minutes). Add chocolate; continue beating, scraping bowl often, until well mixed (1 to 2 minutes). Pour chocolate mixture into prepared pie crust. Bake for 25 to 35 minutes or until center is just set. Cool; sprinkle with reserved 1/3 cup crust mixture. Refrigerate at least 2 hours. **YIELD:** 8 servings.

Nutrition Information (1 serving): Calories 580; Protein 10g; Carbohydrate 38g; Fat 45g; Cholesterol 135mg; Sodium 270mg.

Black Forest Pie

*This fudge brownie pie is topped with
sour cream and cherries.*

Preparation time: 45 minutes • Bake time: 50 minutes • Chilling time: 2 hours

Single crust pie pastry*

Filling
**3/4 cup
  LAND O LAKES® Butter**
3/4 cup sugar
**6 tablespoons unsweetened
  cocoa**
**2/3 cup ground blanched
  almonds**
2 tablespoons all-purpose flour
3 eggs, separated
2 tablespoons water
1/4 cup sugar

Topping
**1/3 cup LAND O LAKES®
  Light Sour Cream
  or dairy sour cream**
2 tablespoons sugar
1/2 teaspoon vanilla
1 cup canned cherry pie filling

Glaze
**1/2 cup semi-sweet real
  chocolate chips**
1 1/2 teaspoons shortening

Heat oven to 350°. Place pastry in 9-inch pie pan. Crimp or flute crust; set aside. In 2-quart saucepan melt 3/4 cup butter over medium heat (3 to 5 minutes). Stir in 3/4 cup sugar and 6 tablespoons cocoa. Remove from heat; cool 5 minutes. Stir in almonds and flour. Stir in egg yolks, one at a time, until well mixed. Stir in 2 tablespoons water. In small mixer bowl beat egg whites at high speed, scraping bowl often, until foamy. Continue beating, gradually adding 1/4 cup sugar, until soft peaks form (30 to 60 seconds). Fold chocolate mixture into egg whites just until blended.

Pour into prepared pie shell. Bake for 35 to 45 minutes or until wooden pick inserted in center comes out clean. Cool 5 minutes. In medium bowl stir together all topping ingredients <u>except</u> cherry pie filling. Spread over warm pie; top with spoonfuls of cherry pie filling. Return pie to oven for 5 minutes. In 1-quart saucepan melt chocolate chips and shortening over low heat, stirring constantly, until melted (2 to 3 minutes). Drizzle over pie. Refrigerate at least 2 hours. **YIELD:** 10 servings.

*See crust recipe on page 66.

Nutrition Information (1 serving): Calories 460; Protein 6g; Carbohydrate 47g; Fat 30g; Cholesterol 120mg; Sodium 280mg.

Chocolate-Laced Pecan Pie

*Two all-time favorites, pecan pie and chocolate,
come together in this extra-rich pie.*

Preparation time: 30 minutes • Baking time: 45 minutes • Chilling time: 4 hours • (pictured)

Crust

1 cup all-purpose flour

1/8 teaspoon salt

1/3 cup
  LAND O LAKES® Butter or
  shortening

3 to 4 tablespoons cold water

Filling

2/3 cup sugar

1/3 cup
  LAND O LAKES® Butter,
  melted

1 cup light corn syrup

3 eggs

1/2 teaspoon salt

1 cup pecan halves

1/2 cup semi-sweet real
  chocolate chips

Pecan halves

Semi-sweet real chocolate
  chips, melted

Sweetened whipped cream

Heat oven to 375°. In large bowl stir together flour and 1/8 teaspoon salt. Cut in 1/3 cup butter until crumbly. With fork mix in water until flour is moistened. Shape into a ball. On lightly floured surface roll pastry ball into 12-inch circle. Place in 9-inch pie pan. Crimp or flute crust; set aside. In small mixer bowl combine sugar, 1/3 cup butter, corn syrup, eggs and 1/2 teaspoon salt. Beat at medium speed, scraping bowl often, until well mixed (1 to 2 minutes). By hand, stir in 1 cup pecans and 1/2 cup chocolate chips. Pour into prepared crust; if desired, turn pecan halves right side up. Cover pie loosely with aluminum foil. Bake for 30 minutes. Remove aluminum foil; continue baking for 10 to 15 minutes or until filling is set. If browning too quickly, re-cover with aluminum foil. Cool; refrigerate at least 4 hours or until ready to serve. If desired, dip additional pecan halves halfway in melted chocolate chips; refrigerate until set. Serve pie with sweetened whipped cream; garnish with dipped pecan halves.
YIELD: 8 servings.

TIP: If desired, omit semi-sweet chocolate chips for a traditional pecan pie.

*Nutrition Information (1 serving): Calories 640; Protein 6g; Carbohydrate 76g; Fat 37g;
Cholesterol 132mg; Sodium 380mg.*

Chocolate Macadamia Nut Pie

*Macadamia nuts and chocolate combine in this
sinfully rich pie.*

Preparation time: 1 hour • Baking time: 1 hour 5 minutes • Chilling time: 4 hours

Crust

1 cup all-purpose flour
1/8 teaspoon salt
1/3 cup shortening
3 to 4 tablespoons cold water

Filling

2/3 cup sugar
1/3 cup
   LAND O LAKES® Butter,
   melted
1 cup dark <u>or</u> light corn syrup
3 eggs
1/2 teaspoon salt
2 (3 1/2 ounce) jars coarsely
   chopped salted macadamia
   nuts, <u>reserve 8 nuts</u>
4 (1 ounce) squares semi-sweet
   baking chocolate, melted

Candied pineapple slices
Semi-sweet chocolate, melted
Sweetened whipped cream

Heat oven to 375°. In medium bowl combine flour and 1/8 teaspoon salt. Cut in shortening until crumbly. With fork mix in water until flour is moistened; shape into ball. On lightly floured surface roll into 12-inch circle. Place in 9-inch pie pan. Crimp or flute crust; set aside. In small mixer bowl combine sugar, butter, corn syrup, eggs and 1/2 teaspoon salt. Beat at medium speed, scraping bowl often, until well mixed (1 to 2 minutes). By hand, stir in nuts and 4 ounces melted chocolate. Pour into prepared pie shell. Bake for 55 to 65 minutes or until filling is set. Cool; refrigerate at least 4 hours or until ready to serve. If desired, cut candied pineapple slices in half; dip slices halfway into melted chocolate. Refrigerate until set. Serve pie with sweetened whipped cream; garnish with dipped pineapple slices and reserved macadamia nuts. **YIELD:** 8 servings.

VARIATION

<u>Chocolate Peanut Pie</u>: Substitute 1 1/2 cups coarsely chopped salted cocktail peanuts for 2 (3 1/2 ounce) jars coarsely chopped salted macadamia nuts.

Nutrition Information (1 serving): Calories 660; Protein 7g; Carbohydrate 71g; Fat 41g; Cholesterol 100mg; Sodium 300mg.

Decadent Chocolate Pie

Toasted hazelnuts add extra flavor to this decadent pie.

Preparation time: 1 hour • Baking time: 30 minutes

Crust
3/4 cup all-purpose flour

3/4 cup ground toasted
   hazelnuts <u>or</u> filberts

3 tablespoons firmly packed
   brown sugar

1/2 cup cold
   LAND O LAKES® Butter,
   cut into 1/2-inch pieces

2 to 3 tablespoons cold water

Filling
1 (6 ounce) package (1 cup)
   semi-sweet real chocolate
   chips

1/3 cup
   LAND O LAKES® Butter

2/3 cup chopped toasted
   hazelnuts <u>or</u> filberts

1/3 cup sugar

3 eggs, separated

1/2 teaspoon cream of tartar

1/4 teaspoon salt

Topping
Sweetened whipped cream

Raspberries

Heat oven to 350°. In medium bowl combine flour, 3/4 cup hazelnuts and brown sugar. Cut in 1/2 cup butter until crumbly. With fork mix in water just until flour is moistened. Shape into ball; flatten ball. With floured hands, press crust mixture on bottom and up sides of 10-inch deep dish pie pan; set aside. In 1-quart saucepan melt chocolate chips and 1/3 cup butter; cool. In medium bowl stir together 2/3 cup hazelnuts, sugar and egg yolks. In small mixer bowl beat egg whites, cream of tartar and salt until soft peaks form (1 to 2 minutes).

Continue beating on low speed, gradually adding egg yolk mixture to egg whites, until well mixed (1 to 2 minutes). By hand, gently fold in chocolate mixture until well mixed. Pour into prepared crust. Bake for 25 to 30 minutes or until just set in center and wooden pick inserted in center comes out clean. If browning too quickly, cover edge of crust with 2-inch strip aluminum foil. Cool completely. To serve, garnish with sweetened whipped cream and raspberries. **YIELD:** 8 servings.

Nutrition Information (1 serving): Calories 530; Protein 7g; Carbohydrate 38g; Fat 42g; Cholesterol 130mg; Sodium 290mg.

Chocolate Silk Pie

This "smooth as silk" chocolate pie has a chocolate cookie crust — a chocolate lover's delight.

Preparation time: 30 minutes • Chilling time: 3 hours • (pictured)

Crust

1 1/2 cups (about 18) finely
   crushed chocolate
   sandwich cookies
1/4 cup
   LAND O LAKES® Butter,
   melted

Filling

1 cup sugar
3/4 cup
   LAND O LAKES® Butter,
   slightly softened
3 (1 ounce) squares semi-sweet
   baking chocolate, melted,
   cooled
3/4 cup refrigerated
   pasteurized liquid eggs

Sweetened whipped cream
Chocolate curls

In medium bowl stir together crust ingredients. Press on bottom and up sides of 9-inch pie pan. Refrigerate 10 minutes. In small mixer bowl combine sugar and 3/4 cup butter. Beat at medium speed, scraping bowl often, until well mixed (1 to 2 minutes). Add chocolate; continue beating, scraping bowl often, until well mixed (1 to 2 minutes). Add eggs; continue beating, scraping bowl often, until light and fluffy (4 minutes). Spoon into prepared crust. Refrigerate at least 3 hours or until set. Garnish with sweetened whipped cream and chocolate curls. **YIELD:** 8 servings.

Nutrition Information (1 serving): Calories 490; Protein 4g; Carbohydrate 47g; Fat 34g; Cholesterol 90mg; Sodium 390mg.

Chewy Caramel-Brownie Pie

*This brownie pie is exceedingly rich, chewy, gooey and irresistible
when topped with a scoop of ice cream.*

Preparation time: 30 minutes • Baking time: 30 minutes • Standing time: 45 minutes • (pictured)

Brownie
1/2 cup
  LAND O LAKES® Butter
2 (1 ounce) squares
  unsweetened chocolate
1 cup sugar
3/4 cup all-purpose flour
2 eggs, slightly beaten
1/2 teaspoon salt
1/2 teaspoon baking powder
1 teaspoon vanilla

Caramel
8 ounces (30) caramels,
  unwrapped
3 tablespoons whipping cream
1/2 cup chopped pecans
1/4 cup semi-sweet
  chocolate chips

Vanilla ice cream

Heat oven to 350°. In 2-quart saucepan combine butter and unsweetened chocolate. Cook over medium heat, stirring occasionally, until melted (4 to 6 minutes). Stir in all remaining brownie ingredients. Spread batter into greased 9-inch pie pan. Bake for 20 to 25 minutes or until brownie is firm to the touch. Meanwhile, in 1-quart saucepan heat caramels and whipping cream over medium low heat, stirring occasionally, until caramels are melted (5 to 6 minutes). Remove brownie from oven; spread melted caramel mixture over entire baked brownie. Sprinkle with pecans and chocolate chips. Continue baking for 3 to 5 minutes or until caramel mixture is bubbly. Let stand 30 to 45 minutes; cut into wedges. Serve warm with ice cream. **YIELD:** 8 servings.

Nutrition Information (1 serving): Calories 640; Protein 8g; Carbohydrate 79g; Fat 36g; Cholesterol 123mg; Sodium 410mg.

Family Favorites

Crumbles,
cobblers, dumplings,
puddings
and
pandowdy:
The homey names
are as inviting
as their fresh-baked
aromas!

Tea Biscuits With Blushing Raspberries, page 88

Tea Biscuits With Blushing Raspberries

*Light, tender biscuits are topped with
ruby red raspberries.*

Preparation time: 25 minutes • Baking time: 14 minutes • (pictured on page 86)

Biscuits

2 cups all-purpose flour
1/2 cup sugar
1 tablespoon baking powder
1/2 teaspoon salt
2/3 cup
   LAND O LAKES® Butter
1/2 cup whipping cream
2 tablespoons orange juice

Whipped Cream

1 cup whipping cream
2 tablespoons sugar
1 teaspoon vanilla

Raspberry Sauce

1 pint fresh raspberries*
1/3 cup powdered sugar
1/4 cup orange juice

1 pint fresh raspberries

Heat oven to 400°. In large bowl combine flour, 1/2 cup sugar, baking powder and salt. Cut in butter until crumbly. Stir in 1/2 cup whipping cream and 2 tablespoons orange juice just until moistened. Turn dough onto lightly floured surface; knead until smooth (1 minute). Roll out dough to 1/2-inch thickness. With 2-inch scalloped round or heart-shaped cutter, cut out 8 biscuits. Place 1-inch apart on cookie sheet. Bake for 10 to 14 minutes or until lightly browned.

Meanwhile, in chilled small mixer bowl beat chilled 1 cup whipping cream at high speed, scraping bowl often, until soft peaks form. Continue beating, gradually adding 2 tablespoons sugar, until stiff peaks form (1 to 2 minutes). By hand, fold in vanilla. In 5-cup blender container place 1 pint raspberries, powdered sugar and 1/4 cup orange juice. Blend on High speed until pureed (1 to 2 minutes). If desired, strain sauce to remove seeds. Place biscuits in individual dessert dishes. Serve with raspberry sauce, whipped cream and fresh raspberries. **YIELD:** 8 servings.

*1 (10 ounce) package frozen raspberries can be substituted for 1 pint fresh raspberries.

Nutrition Information (1 serving): Calories 520; Protein 5g; Carbohydrate 55g; Fat 33g; Cholesterol 103mg; Sodium 420mg.

Grandma Ruth's Cherry Crumble

*This country-style favorite gets its name from fruit baked
with a crumbly mixture on top.*

Preparation time: 15 minutes • Baking time: 30 minutes

Crumble
1/2 cup all-purpose flour
1/2 cup old-fashioned
   rolled oats
1/3 cup firmly packed
   brown sugar
1/2 teaspoon nutmeg
1/3 cup
   LAND O LAKES® Butter
1/2 cup sliced almonds

Filling
2 (16 ounce) cans pitted tart
   cherries, drained
1/2 cup sugar
1 tablespoon all-purpose flour
1 teaspoon vanilla

Vanilla ice cream

Heat oven to 350°. In large bowl stir together all crumble
ingredients <u>except</u> butter and almonds. Cut in butter until
crumbly; stir in almonds. Set aside. In medium bowl stir together
all filling ingredients <u>except</u> ice cream. Place about 1/2 cup filling
in each of 6 (6 ounce) custard cups or ramekins. Sprinkle each cup
with about <u>1/4 cup</u> crumble mixture; place cups on 15x10x1-inch
jelly roll pan. Bake for 25 to 30 minutes or until bubbly and lightly
browned. Serve warm with vanilla ice cream. **YIELD:** 6 servings.

TIP: Grandma Ruth's Cherry Crumble can be baked in 1 1/2-quart casserole. Bake
for 30 to 35 minutes.

*Nutrition Information (1 serving): Calories 520; Protein 8g; Carbohydrate 77g; Fat 22g;
Cholesterol 58mg; Sodium 170mg.*

Granny's Peaches & Cream Cobbler

This irresistible cobbler brings memories of visits to Grandma's house.

Preparation time: 30 minutes • Baking time: 45 minutes • (pictured)

Filling

1 cup sugar

2 eggs, slightly beaten

2 tablespoons all-purpose flour

1/2 teaspoon nutmeg

4 cups (4 to 6 medium) peeled, sliced fresh peaches*

Cobbler

1 1/2 cups all-purpose flour

2 tablespoons sugar

1 teaspoon baking powder

1/2 teaspoon salt

1/3 cup
   LAND O LAKES® Butter, softened

1 egg, slightly beaten

3 tablespoons milk

3 tablespoons sugar

Whipping cream

Heat oven to 400°. In large bowl stir together all filling ingredients <u>except</u> peaches. Stir in peaches. Pour into 13x9-inch baking pan. In medium bowl stir together all cobbler ingredients <u>except</u> butter, egg and milk. Cut in butter until crumbly. Stir in egg and milk just until moistened. Crumble mixture over peaches; sprinkle with 3 tablespoons sugar. Bake for 40 to 45 minutes or until golden brown and bubbly around edges. Serve with whipping cream. **YIELD:** 8 servings.

*2 (16 ounce) packages sliced frozen peaches can be substituted for 4 cups sliced fresh peaches.

Nutrition Information (1 serving): Calories 410; Protein 6g; Carbohydrate 63g; Fat 16g; Cholesterol 122mg; Sodium 280mg.

Old-Fashioned Banana Bread Pudding

A cozy kind of dessert that's both comforting and scrumptious.

Preparation time: 20 minutes • Baking time: 50 minutes

Bread Pudding

1/4 cup
  LAND O LAKES® Butter

4 cups cubed 1-inch stale
  French or sourdough bread

3 eggs

1/2 cup sugar

2 cups milk

1/2 teaspoon cinnamon

1/2 teaspoon nutmeg

1/4 teaspoon salt

2 teaspoons vanilla

1 cup (2 medium) sliced
  1/4-inch bananas

Sauce

3 tablespoons
  LAND O LAKES® Butter

2 tablespoons sugar

1 tablespoon cornstarch

3/4 cup milk

1/4 cup light corn syrup

1 teaspoon vanilla

Heat oven to 375°. In 2-quart casserole melt 1/4 cup butter in oven (4 to 6 minutes). Stir in bread cubes. In medium bowl slightly beat eggs; stir in all remaining pudding ingredients <u>except</u> bananas. Stir in bananas. Pour over bread cubes; stir to coat. Bake for 40 to 50 minutes or until knife inserted in center comes out clean. Meanwhile, in 1-quart saucepan melt 3 tablespoons butter over medium heat. Stir in sugar and cornstarch; add remaining ingredients <u>except</u> vanilla. Continue cooking, stirring occasionally, until sauce comes to a full boil (3 to 4 minutes). Boil 1 minute. Stir in vanilla. Serve sauce over warm pudding. **YIELD:** 6 servings.

Nutrition Information (1 serving): Calories 450; Protein 10g; Carbohydrate 61g; Fat 19g; Cholesterol 152mg; Sodium 500mg.

Pear Pandowdy

Pandowdy—a traditional favorite—features fresh fruit baked with buttery cinnamon-sugar and topped with biscuits.

Preparation time: 20 minutes • Baking time: 55 minutes

1 cup firmly packed
   brown sugar
1/2 cup
   LAND O LAKES® Butter,
   softened
2 tablespoons all-purpose flour
1/4 teaspoon cinnamon
2 tablespoons lemon juice
5 cups (5 medium) peeled,
   cored, sliced 1/8-inch pears*

Biscuits
1 1/2 cups buttermilk
   baking mix
1/2 cup milk
1 tablespoon sugar
1/4 teaspoon cinnamon

Vanilla ice cream <u>or</u>
   whipping cream

Heat oven to 400°. In large mixer bowl combine brown sugar, butter, flour, 1/4 teaspoon cinnamon and lemon juice. Beat at medium speed, scraping bowl often, until well mixed (1 to 2 minutes). Add pears; toss to coat. Spoon into 2-quart casserole. Cover; bake for 25 to 35 minutes or until pears are crisply tender. Meanwhile, in small bowl combine baking mix and milk; stir until just moistened. Drop dough by spoonfuls onto hot pear mixture to make 9 biscuits. In small bowl stir together sugar and cinnamon. Sprinkle sugar mixture over biscuits. Continue baking, uncovered, for 15 to 20 minutes or until biscuits are lightly browned. Serve warm with ice cream or whipping cream.
YIELD: 9 servings.

*5 cups (5 medium) peeled, cored, sliced 1/8-inch apples can be substituted for 5 cups sliced pears.

Nutrition Information (1 serving): Calories 480; Protein 5g; Carbohydrate 69g, Fat 21g, Cholesterol 59mg; Sodium 370mg.

Apple Dumplings & Brandy Sauce

*A tender butter crust, baked to a golden brown, surrounds
these pecan-filled apple dumplings smothered in a rich sauce.*

Preparation time: 1 hour • Baking time: 50 minutes • (pictured)

Dumplings

2 cups all-purpose flour
1/4 teaspoon salt
1/2 cup
  LAND O LAKES® Butter,
  cut into pieces
2/3 cup LAND O LAKES®
  Light Sour Cream
  <u>or</u> dairy sour cream
6 medium tart cooking apples,
  cored, peeled
1/3 cup sugar
1/3 cup chopped pecans
2 tablespoons
  LAND O LAKES® Butter,
  softened
Milk

Sauce

1/2 cup firmly packed
  brown sugar
2 tablespoons
  LAND O LAKES® Butter
1/2 cup whipping cream
1 tablespoon brandy*

Heat oven to 400°. In medium bowl stir together flour and salt. Cut in 1/2 cup butter until mixture forms coarse crumbs. With fork, stir in Light Sour Cream until mixture leaves sides of bowl and forms a ball. On lightly floured surface roll dough into 19x12-inch rectangle. Cut 1-inch strip off 19-inch end; reserve. Cut remaining dough into 6 (6-inch) squares. Place apple in center of each square. In small bowl stir together sugar, pecans and 2 tablespoons butter. Stuff <u>1 1/2 tablespoons</u> of mixture into cored center of each apple. Fold dough up around apple; seal seams well. Place, seam side down, on greased 15x10x1-inch jelly roll pan. Brush dough with milk; prick dough with fork.

Cut leaf designs out of reserved 1-inch strip of dough. Brush with milk; place on wrapped apples. Bake for 35 to 50 minutes or until apples are fork-tender. If crust browns too quickly, cover with aluminum foil. In 1-quart saucepan combine all sauce ingredients. Cook over medium heat, stirring occasionally, until mixture comes to a full boil (3 to 4 minutes). Serve sauce over warm dumplings. **YIELD:** 6 servings.

*1 teaspoon brandy extract can be substituted for 1 tablespoon brandy.

Nutrition Information (1 serving): Calories 690; Protein 7g; Carbohydrate 87g; Fat 37g; Cholesterol 96mg; Sodium 360mg.

Caramel Rum Fruit Dip

Rich and creamy, this dip is an indulgent way to dress up fruit.

Preparation time: 30 minutes

1/2 cup
   LAND O LAKES® Butter
1 (14 ounce) package caramels,
   unwrapped
1/4 cup chopped pecans
1 tablespoon milk
1 tablespoon rum*

Cut-up fresh fruit

In 2-quart saucepan melt butter and caramels over low heat, stirring occasionally, until caramels are melted (12 to 15 minutes). Stir in pecans, milk and rum. Stir vigorously to incorporate butter. Keep warm; use as a dip for cut-up fresh fruit or serve over ice cream. **YIELD:** 1 1/2 cups.

*1 teaspoon rum extract can be substituted for 1 tablespoon rum.

Nutrition Information (1 tablespoon dip): Calories 110; Protein 1g; Carbohydrate 13g; Fat 6g; Cholesterol 10mg; Sodium 75mg.

Individual Fruit-Filled Meringues

These heart-shaped meringues showcase a cloud of whipped cream and a colorful arrangement of fresh fruit.

Preparation time: 30 minutes • Baking time: 1 hour • Cooling time: 1 hour 30 minutes

Meringues
4 egg whites
2 teaspoons cornstarch
1/4 teaspoon cream of tartar
1 teaspoon lemon juice
1 cup sugar
1/3 cup powdered sugar

Whipped Cream
1 cup whipping cream
1/4 cup sugar
1 teaspoon vanilla

1 cup sliced fresh strawberries
1 cup 1-inch pieces fresh
   pineapple
1 kiwi, cut into 6 slices

Heat oven to 275°. In large mixer bowl beat egg whites, cornstarch, cream of tartar and lemon juice at high speed, scraping bowl often, until soft peaks form (1 to 2 minutes). Continue beating, gradually adding 1 cup sugar and powdered sugar, until glossy and stiff peaks form (6 to 8 minutes). On brown paper or parchment paper-lined cookie sheet, shape or pipe 6 (about 4-inch) individual heart-shaped or round meringues, building up sides. Bake for 1 hour. Turn off oven; leave meringues in oven with door closed for 1 hour. Finish cooling meringues at room temperature. In chilled small mixer bowl beat chilled whipping cream at high speed, scraping bowl often, until soft peaks form. Continue beating, gradually adding 1/4 cup sugar, until stiff peaks form (1 to 2 minutes). By hand, fold in vanilla. Fill meringue shells with whipped cream; top with strawberries, pineapple and kiwi. **YIELD:** 6 servings.

Nutrition Information (1 serving): Calories 370; Protein 4g; Carbohydrate 57g; Fat 15g; Cholesterol 54mg; Sodium 55mg.

Glazed Fruit Cups

*Pretty pastry cups are filled with
orange–flavored fruits.*

Preparation time: 1 hour • Baking time: 18 minutes • (pictured)

Cups

2 cups all-purpose flour

1/4 teaspoon salt

2/3 cup
   LAND O LAKES® Butter

4 to 5 tablespoons cold water

1 teaspoon grated orange peel

Filling

1/4 cup sugar

2 teaspoons cornstarch

1/2 cup orange juice

2 tablespoons
   LAND O LAKES® Butter

1 1/2 cups cut-up fresh fruit
   (bananas, grapes,
   raspberries, strawberries,
   peaches, etc.)

Red raspberry preserves,
   melted

Heat oven to 400°. In large bowl stir together flour and salt. Cut in 2/3 cup butter until crumbly; with fork, stir in water and orange peel until dough leaves sides of bowl and forms a ball. Roll out dough on well-floured surface to 1/8-inch thickness. Cut into 10 (4 1/2-inch) circles. Fit pastry into muffin cups; flute edges. With fork, prick bottom and sides of each cup. Bake for 14 to 18 minutes or until lightly browned. Cool; remove from pan. In 2-quart saucepan stir together sugar and cornstarch. Add orange juice. Cook over medium heat, stirring occasionally, until mixture comes to a full boil (5 to 8 minutes). Boil 2 minutes. Remove from heat. Stir in 2 tablespoons butter until melted. Gently stir in fruit. Spoon fruit mixture into each cup. If desired, top each cup with about 1 teaspoon melted raspberry preserves. **YIELD:** 10 servings.

TIP: Pastry cups can be made one day ahead.

Nutrition Information (1 serving): Calories 280; Protein 3g; Carbohydrate 34g; Fat 15g; Cholesterol 39mg; Sodium 203mg.

Raspberry Cream Cheese Turnovers

*Serve this raspberry cream pastry for
brunch or dessert.*

Preparation time: 1 hour • Chilling time: 30 minutes • Baking time: 25 minutes • (pictured)

Pastry

2 1/2 cups all-purpose flour
2/3 cup
   LAND O LAKES® Butter
1/2 cup LAND O LAKES®
   Light Sour Cream
   <u>or</u> dairy sour cream
4 to 6 tablespoons water

Filling

1 (3 ounce) package cream
   cheese, softened
1 egg yolk
2 tablespoons sugar
1 teaspoon all-purpose flour
1/2 teaspoon almond extract
1/4 cup raspberry preserves

Topping

2 tablespoons
   LAND O LAKES® Butter,
   melted
2 tablespoons sugar

Glaze

1/2 cup powdered sugar
1 tablespoon milk
1/4 teaspoon almond extract

In large bowl cut 2/3 cup butter into 2 1/2 cups flour until crumbly; stir in Light Sour Cream. With fork mix in water, 1 tablespoon at a time, until flour mixture is moistened. Divide dough in half; shape into 2 balls and flatten. Cover; refrigerate 30 minutes. <u>Heat oven to 400°</u>.

In medium bowl stir together all filling ingredients <u>except</u> raspberry preserves until smooth. On lightly floured surface roll out half of dough into 12x8-inch rectangle. Cut into six 4-inch squares. In center of each square place <u>2 teaspoons</u> filling and <u>1 teaspoon</u> raspberry preserves. Fold one corner of dough over filling to form a triangle. Seal edges with fork. Place on lightly greased cookie sheets. Repeat with remaining dough and filling. Brush tops of turnovers with 2 tablespoons melted butter; sprinkle with 2 tablespoons sugar. Bake for 20 to 25 minutes or until light golden brown. In small bowl stir together all glaze ingredients until smooth; drizzle over warm turnovers. Serve warm.
YIELD: 12 servings.

Nutrition Information (1 serving): Calories 290; Protein 4g; Carbohydrate 34g; Fat 16g; Cholesterol 61mg; Sodium 150mg.

Orange Pecan Delight

This tender, moist dessert bakes while you eat dinner.

Preparation time: 45 minutes • Baking time: 50 minutes

1/4 cup
   LAND O LAKES® Butter
1/3 cup crushed vanilla wafers
1/4 cup all-purpose flour
1/2 cup milk
1/2 cup orange juice
4 eggs, separated
2 tablespoons sugar
1/3 cup sugar
1/2 teaspoon vanilla
1/2 cup finely chopped pecans

1 cup whipping cream
2 tablespoons sugar
2 teaspoons grated
   orange peel

Grease bottoms only of 8 individual souffle dishes or custard cups. In 2-quart saucepan melt butter over low heat. Stir in crushed vanilla wafers and flour; gradually stir in milk and juice. Cook over medium heat, stirring constantly, until mixture thickens and comes to a full boil (6 to 8 minutes). Remove from heat; cool 20 minutes. <u>Heat oven to 325°</u>. In small mixer bowl beat egg whites at high speed, scraping bowl often, until soft peaks form (1 to 2 minutes). Continue beating, gradually adding 2 tablespoons sugar, until stiff peaks form (1 to 2 minutes); set aside.

In large mixer bowl combine egg yolks, 1/3 cup sugar and vanilla. Beat at medium speed, scraping bowl often, until thickened and lemon-colored (2 to 3 minutes). Stir pecans and wafer mixture into yolks. Fold in egg whites just until mixed. Spoon into prepared dishes. Place dishes in 2 (9-inch square) baking pans; place in oven. Pour 1 inch hot water into pans. Bake for 40 to 50 minutes or until knife inserted in center comes out clean. Meanwhile, in small chilled mixer bowl beat chilled whipping cream at high speed, scraping bowl often, until soft peaks form. Continue beating, gradually adding 2 tablespoons sugar and orange peel, until stiff peaks form. Serve hot dessert immediately with orange whipped cream.

YIELD: 8 servings.

TIP: 1 1/2-quart souffle dish can be substituted for 8 individual souffle dishes. Bake for 75 to 90 minutes or until knife inserted halfway between edge and center comes out clean.

Nutrition Information (1 serving): Calories 350; Protein 6g; Carbohydrate 26g; Fat 25g; Cholesterol 165mg; Sodium 120mg.

Bananas Foster With Crepes

Buttery crepes are served in a rich
banana-rum sauce.

Preparation time: 45 minutes • Cooking time: 12 minutes

Crepes
3/4 cup all-purpose flour
1 1/2 teaspoons sugar
1/4 teaspoon baking powder
1/4 teaspoon salt
1 cup milk
1 egg
1 tablespoon
  LAND O LAKES® Butter,
  melted
1/4 teaspoon vanilla
1 teaspoon
  LAND O LAKES® Butter

Sauce
1/2 cup
  LAND O LAKES® Butter
1 3/4 cups powdered sugar
1/4 cup milk
1/2 teaspoon cinnamon
2 tablespoons rum*
3 medium bananas,
  sliced 1/4-inch
2 tablespoons lemon juice

In small mixer bowl combine flour, sugar, baking powder and salt. Add remaining crepe ingredients <u>except</u> 1 teaspoon butter. Beat at medium speed, scraping bowl often, until smooth (1 to 2 minutes). Melt 1 teaspoon butter in 6 or 8-inch skillet until sizzling. For <u>each</u> of 6 crepes, pour about 1/4 cup batter into skillet; immediately rotate skillet until thin film covers bottom. Cook over medium heat until lightly browned (2 to 3 minutes). Run wide spatula around edge to loosen; turn. Continue cooking until lightly browned (2 to 3 minutes). Place crepes on plate, placing waxed paper between each. Cover crepes; set aside.

In 10-inch skillet melt 1/2 cup butter over medium heat. Stir in powdered sugar, 1/4 cup milk, cinnamon and rum. In small bowl combine bananas and lemon juice; toss to coat bananas. Gently stir bananas into sauce in skillet. Fold each crepe in half; fold in half again to form triangles. Arrange crepes in skillet; spoon sauce over crepes. Cook over medium heat, spooning sauce over crepes occasionally, until heated through (4 to 6 minutes). Serve immediately. **YIELD:** 6 servings.

*1 teaspoon rum extract can be substituted for 2 tablespoons rum.

Nutrition Information (1 serving): Calories 440; Protein 5g; Carbohydrate 59g; Fat 20g; Cholesterol 88mg; Sodium 320mg.

Poached Pears With Raspberry & Chocolate Sauce

Ripe pears poached in wine are complemented
with two sauces.

Preparation time: 30 minutes • Cooking time: 43 minutes • Cooling time: 20 minutes • (pictured)

Pears

1/3 cup sugar

1 1/2 cups sauterne wine
   <u>or</u> white grape juice

1 1/2 cups water

4 medium ripe pears, peeled,
   leave stems on

Sauce

1 (10 ounce) package frozen
   raspberries in syrup, thawed

2 teaspoons cornstarch

1 cup chocolate flavored syrup

4 teaspoons chopped
   slivered almonds

In Dutch oven combine all pear ingredients. Cook over medium-high heat until mixture comes to a full boil (4 to 5 minutes). Reduce heat to medium; cover. Continue cooking, basting often, until pears are fork tender (20 to 30 minutes). Cool 15 minutes; drain. Cover pears; refrigerate until serving time or serve at room temperature. Meanwhile, press raspberries through strainer; discard seeds. (Strain raspberries again if seeds still remain.) In 1-quart saucepan, with wire whisk, stir together strained raspberries and cornstarch. Cook over medium heat, stirring constantly, until mixture comes to a full boil (3 to 6 minutes). Boil, stirring constantly, until slightly thickened (2 minutes). Remove from heat. Cool 5 minutes; stir. Cover; refrigerate until serving time. To serve, spoon <u>2 to 3 tablespoons</u> chocolate syrup onto each of 4 individual serving plates. Cut thin slice off bottom of each pear. Stand pears upright in chocolate sauce. Spoon <u>1 to 2 tablespoons</u> raspberry sauce over top of each pear, allowing sauce to drizzle down sides of pear; sprinkle with <u>1 teaspoon</u> almonds. **YIELD:** 4 servings.

Nutrition Information (1 serving): Calories 390; Protein 3g; Carbohydrate 94g; Fat 3g;
Cholesterol 0mg; Sodium 75mg.

Banana Split Squares

*A new twist on banana splits—
sure to please a crowd.*

Preparation time: 30 minutes • Cooking time: 26 minutes • Freezing time: 7 hours

Crust

1/2 cup
   LAND O LAKES® Butter
2 cups graham cracker crumbs
1/4 cup sugar

Filling

3 bananas, sliced 1/4-inch
1/2 gallon vanilla ice cream,
   slightly softened
1 cup chopped walnuts

Sauce

2 cups powdered sugar
1/2 cup
   LAND O LAKES® Butter
1 (12 ounce) can evaporated
   milk
1 (6 ounce) package (1 cup)
   semi-sweet real chocolate
   chips
1 teaspoon vanilla

Topping

1 cup whipping cream

Maraschino cherries

In 2-quart saucepan melt 1/2 cup butter. Stir in crumbs and sugar. Press crumb mixture on bottom of 13x9-inch pan. Layer banana slices over crumb mixture. Spread ice cream over bananas. Sprinkle with chopped nuts. Cover; freeze until firm (about 4 hours). Meanwhile, in 2-quart saucepan combine all sauce ingredients. Cook over low heat, stirring occasionally, until mixture thickens and comes to a full boil (20 to 25 minutes). Boil 1 minute. Cool completely; pour evenly over ice cream. Cover; freeze until firm (about 3 hours). In chilled bowl beat chilled whipping cream at high speed, scraping bowl often, until soft peaks form. Spread over sauce. If desired, garnish with maraschino cherries. Serve immediately or freeze until served. **YIELD:** 15 servings.

Nutrition Information (1 serving): Calories 580; Protein 8g; Carbohydrate 58g; Fat 38g; Cholesterol 94mg; Sodium 296mg.

Strawberry Trifle

Layers of fresh strawberries, pudding and whipping cream make this dessert as pretty as it is good to eat.

Preparation time: 45 minutes • Chilling time: 2 hours

1 (3 1/2 ounce) package vanilla flavored instant pudding and pie filling

1 (8 ounce) carton (1 cup) LAND O LAKES® Light Sour Cream or dairy sour cream

1 cup milk

1 teaspoon grated orange peel

2 cups (1 pint) whipping cream, whipped

1/2 (10-inch) tube angel food cake, cut into bite-size pieces

2 pints fresh strawberries, hulled, sliced

In large mixer bowl place instant pudding, Light Sour Cream, milk and orange peel. Beat at low speed, scraping bowl often, until thick and well mixed (1 to 2 minutes). By hand, fold in whipped cream. In large serving bowl layer 1/2 of cake pieces, 1/3 strawberries and 1/2 pudding mixture. Repeat layers. Arrange remaining strawberries on top. Cover; refrigerate at least 2 hours. **YIELD:** 8 servings.

Nutrition Information (1 serving): Calories 430; Protein 7g; Carbohydrate 48g; Fat 25g; Cholesterol 88mg; Sodium 319mg.

Apricot-Laced Cream Puffs

*An apricot cream cheese filling provides an interesting twist
to classic cream puffs.*

Preparation time: 1 hour • Baking time: 40 minutes • Cooling time: 30 minutes • (pictured)

Cream Puffs
1 cup water
1/2 cup
   LAND O LAKES® Butter
1 cup all-purpose flour
4 eggs

Apricot Cream
1/2 cup whipping cream
1/4 cup powdered sugar
1 (8 ounce) package
   cream cheese, softened
1/2 teaspoon ginger
2 tablespoons apricot
   preserves

1/2 cup apricot preserves,
   melted
Powdered sugar

Heat oven to 400°. In 2-quart saucepan bring water and butter to a full boil. Stir in flour. Cook over low heat, stirring vigorously, until mixture forms a ball. Add eggs, one at a time, beating until smooth. Drop about 1/3 cup dough 3 inches apart onto cookie sheet. Bake for 35 to 40 minutes or until puffed and golden brown. Cool completely. In chilled small mixer bowl beat chilled whipping cream at high speed, scraping bowl often, until soft peaks form. Continue beating, gradually adding 1/4 cup powdered sugar, until stiff peaks form (1 to 2 minutes). Add remaining apricot cream ingredients <u>except</u> 1/2 cup apricot preserves and powdered sugar. Continue beating, scraping bowl often, until smooth (2 to 3 minutes). Cut off cream puff tops; pull out any filaments of soft dough. Fill puffs with apricot cream; replace tops. Drizzle with melted apricot preserves; sprinkle with powdered sugar. **YIELD:** 8 servings.

Nutrition Information (1 serving): Calories 430; Protein 7g; Carbohydrate 34g; Fat 30g; Cholesterol 189mg; Sodium 240mg.

Chocolate Raspberry Mousse

*Serve this delicious chocolate raspberry mousse
in pretty parfait glasses.*

Preparation time: 20 minutes • (pictured)

1/2 cup
   LAND O LAKES® Butter,
   softened
1/3 cup sugar
2 (1 ounce) squares semi-sweet
   baking chocolate, melted,
   cooled
1/2 cup refrigerated
   pasteurized liquid egg
2 teaspoons raspberry
   liqueur, if desired
1 cup fresh raspberries

In small mixer bowl combine butter and sugar. Beat at medium speed, scraping bowl often, until very light and fluffy (2 to 3 minutes). Add chocolate; continue beating, scraping bowl often, until well mixed (1 to 2 minutes). Add egg; continue beating, scraping bowl often, until very light and fluffy (4 to 5 minutes). By hand, stir in raspberry liqueur. To serve, place several raspberries in bottom of each of 4 parfait glasses. Top with <u>1/4 cup</u> chocolate mousse. Add several more raspberries. Top with <u>1/4 cup</u> chocolate mousse. Garnish with raspberries. Store refrigerated. **YIELD:** 4 servings.

Nutrition Information (1 serving): Calories 400; Protein 4g; Carbohydrate 30g; Fat 31g; Cholesterol 85mg; Sodium 295mg.

Layered Pralines & Creme

A crunchy praline mixture complements this creamy custard.

Preparation time: 30 minutes • Baking time: 14 minutes • Cooling time: 30 minutes • Cooking time: 10 minutes Chilling time: 2 hours • (pictured)

Crunch Mixture

1/4 cup
  LAND O LAKES® Butter
1/2 cup bite-size crispy rice
  cereal squares
1/2 cup flaked coconut
1/2 cup slivered almonds
1/2 cup firmly packed
  brown sugar
1/2 cup chopped pecans

Custard

1/2 cup sugar
1 cup milk
1 egg, slightly beaten
1 tablespoon cornstarch
1 teaspoon vanilla
1 cup whipping cream,
  whipped

Heat oven to 325°. In 15x10x1-inch jelly roll pan melt butter in oven (4 to 5 minutes). Add remaining crunch mixture ingredients; stir well to coat. Bake for 12 to 14 minutes, stirring occasionally, until golden brown. Cool completely; crumble cereal with fingers. In 2-quart saucepan combine all custard ingredients <u>except</u> vanilla and whipped cream. Cook over medium heat, stirring often, until mixture comes to a full boil (7 to 9 minutes). Boil 1 minute. Remove from heat; stir in vanilla. Cover surface with plastic food wrap; refrigerate until cooled completely (1 to 2 hours). Fold whipped cream into custard mixture. Just before serving, alternate layers of custard and crunch mixture into dessert glasses.
YIELD: 6 servings.

Nutrition Information (1 serving): Calories 540; Protein 6g; Carbohydrate 48g; Fat 38g; Cholesterol 114mg; Sodium 150mg.

Chocolate Truffle Pudding

Indulge in this truffle-like pudding to satisfy
chocolate cravings.

Preparation time: 15 minutes • Cooking time: 15 minutes • Cooling time: 30 minutes • Chilling time: 2 hours • (pictured)

1 cup milk

1 cup whipping cream

1/2 cup sugar

3 tablespoons unsweetened
   cocoa

2 tablespoons cornstarch

3/4 cup semi-sweet real
   chocolate chips

1 egg, slightly beaten

2 egg yolks, slightly beaten

2 tablespoons
   LAND O LAKES® Butter

1 teaspoon vanilla

Sweetened whipped cream

Zest of orange peel

Unsweetened cocoa

In 2-quart saucepan stir together milk and whipping cream. Cook over medium heat until warm (3 to 5 minutes). In small bowl stir together sugar, 3 tablespoons cocoa and cornstarch. Gradually add to milk mixture. Add all remaining ingredients <u>except</u> whipped cream, zest of orange peel and cocoa. Continue cooking, stirring constantly, until pudding just begins to thicken (5 to 10 minutes). Pour pudding into 6 or 8 (1/2 cup) individual dessert dishes. Cool 30 minutes. Cover; refrigerate at least 2 hours. Pipe with sweetened whipped cream; top with zest of orange peel and sprinkle with cocoa. **YIELD:** 8 servings.

Nutrition Information (1 serving): Calories 310; Protein 4g; Carbohydrate 27g; Fat 23g; Cholesterol 130mg; Sodium 80mg.

Orange Creme Caramel

*Rich, velvety custard forms its own caramel
sauce as it bakes.*

Preparation time: 45 minutes • Baking time: 45 minutes • Standing time: 30 minutes • (pictured)

1/2 cup sugar

2 1/2 cups milk

1/3 cup sugar

3 eggs

1 tablespoon orange flavored
   liqueur <u>or</u> orange juice

Nutmeg

Pear, red apple,
   nectarine <u>or</u> berries

Orange flavored liqueur
   <u>or</u> orange juice

Heat oven to 350°. In 1-quart saucepan cook 1/2 cup sugar over medium heat, stirring constantly, until golden brown and forms a caramel syrup (6 to 8 minutes). Divide caramel syrup between 6 (6 ounce) custard cups or fluted ramekins. Let stand 10 minutes. Meanwhile, in 2-quart saucepan heat milk over medium heat, stirring occasionally, until hot (4 to 5 minutes). (Do not boil.) In medium bowl, with wire whisk, gradually stir sugar into eggs; gradually whisk hot milk into egg mixture. Stir in 1 tablespoon orange flavored liqueur. Pour about <u>1/2 cup</u> milk mixture into each custard cup; sprinkle with nutmeg. Place custard cups in 13x9-inch baking pan; pour 2 inches hot water into pan. Bake for 40 to 45 minutes or until knife inserted in center of custards comes out clean. Let stand 30 minutes. Serve warm or cover; refrigerate. Just before serving, cut choice of fruit into very thin slices; sprinkle with orange flavored liqueur. On individual dessert plates unmold creme caramel; garnish with sliced fruit or berries. **YIELD:** 6 servings.

Nutrition Information (1 serving): Calories 200; Protein 7g; Carbohydrate 35g; Fat 5g; Cholesterol 115mg; Sodium 83mg.

Double Fudge Brownie Baked Alaska

*A classic dessert with a new twist
—chocolate in all three layers.*

Preparation time: 45 minutes • Baking time: 55 minutes • Freezing time: 4 hours

Brownie
3/4 cup firmly packed
   brown sugar
1/2 cup
   LAND O LAKES® Butter,
   softened
3/4 cup all-purpose flour
1 1/2 cups miniature
   semi-sweet real chocolate
   chips, melted
3 eggs

Filling
1/2 gallon your favorite
   chocolate flavor
   ice cream, softened

Meringue
6 egg whites
1/4 teaspoon salt
1 teaspoon vanilla
3/4 cup sugar
1/2 cup miniature semi-sweet
   real chocolate chips

Heat oven to 350°. Grease 9-inch round cake pan. Line with aluminum foil, leaving excess aluminum foil over edges; grease aluminum foil. Set aside. In large mixer bowl combine brown sugar and butter. Beat at medium speed, scraping bowl often, until smooth (2 to 3 minutes). Add flour, chocolate and eggs. Continue beating, scraping bowl often, until well mixed (2 to 3 minutes). Pour into prepared pan. Bake for 40 to 50 minutes or until wooden pick inserted halfway between edge and center comes out clean. Cool completely; remove from pan by lifting aluminum foil.

Meanwhile, line 2 1/2-quart bowl with aluminum foil; pack ice cream into bowl. Cover; freeze until firm (3 to 4 hours). Heat oven to 450°. In large mixer bowl beat egg whites at high speed, scraping bowl often, until soft peaks form (1 to 2 minutes). Add salt and vanilla. Continue beating, gradually adding sugar, until stiff peaks form (2 to 3 minutes). Fold in 1/2 cup chocolate chips. Place brownie on oven-proof plate. Invert ice cream onto brownie; remove bowl and aluminum foil. Spread meringue evenly over entire surface, covering any holes. Bake for 3 to 5 minutes or until lightly browned. Serve immediately. **YIELD:** 12 servings.

Nutrition Information (1 serving): Calories 550; Protein 9g; Carbohydrate 69g; Fat 29g; Cholesterol 114mg; Sodium 250mg.

Salted Peanut Ice Cream Squares

**A sure hit, the flavors in this frozen dessert are similar
to a popular candy bar.**

Preparation time: 30 minutes • Freezing time: 4 hours

1/2 cup light corn syrup
1/2 cup chunky style
  peanut butter
3 cups crisp rice cereal

1/2 gallon vanilla ice cream,
  slightly softened*
1 cup chopped salted
  peanuts

Caramel ice cream topping

In large bowl stir together corn syrup and peanut butter. Stir in cereal. Press on bottom of buttered 13x9-inch pan; freeze until firm (about 10 minutes). Spread ice cream on top of crust; sprinkle with chopped peanuts. Pat into ice cream. Cover; freeze until firm (2 to 4 hours). To serve, in 1-quart saucepan heat caramel topping. Cut ice cream into squares; serve caramel topping over ice cream. **YIELD:** 12 servings.

* 1/2 gallon chocolate chip, praline pecan or your favorite flavor ice cream can be substituted for 1/2 gallon vanilla ice cream.

Nutrition Information (1 serving): Calories 410; Protein 10g; Carbohydrate 48g; Fat 21g; Cholesterol 40mg; Sodium 294mg.

Chocolate Hazelnut Truffle Dessert

Serve a thin slice of this rich, dense chocolate dessert
with a creamy custard sauce.

Preparation time: 1 hour • Freezing time: 8 hours • Cooking time: 11 minutes • (pictured)

Truffle Dessert
1 cup whipping cream
1/4 cup
　LAND O LAKES® Butter
2 (8 ounce) bars semi-sweet
　chocolate
4 egg yolks
3/4 cup powdered sugar
3 tablespoons rum <u>or</u>
　orange juice
1 cup coarsely chopped
　hazelnuts <u>or</u> filberts, toasted

Custard
1 cup whipping cream
1/4 cup sugar
1 teaspoon cornstarch
3 egg yolks
1 teaspoon vanilla

Garnish
Finely chopped hazelnuts

In 2-quart saucepan combine 1 cup whipping cream, butter and chocolate. Cook over medium heat, stirring occasionally, until chocolate is melted (5 to 7 minutes). With wire whisk stir in 4 egg yolks, one at a time. Continue cooking, stirring constantly, until mixture reaches 160° and thickens slightly (3 to 4 minutes). Remove from heat; whisk in powdered sugar and rum. Stir in hazelnuts. Line 8x4-inch loaf pan with aluminum foil, leaving 1-inch of aluminum foil over each edge. Pour chocolate mixture into prepared pan. Freeze 8 hours or overnight. In 2-quart saucepan cook 1 cup whipping cream over medium heat until mixture just comes to a boil (4 to 6 minutes). Remove from heat.

Meanwhile, in medium bowl combine sugar and cornstarch. Whisk in 3 egg yolks until mixture is light and creamy (3 to 4 minutes). Gradually whisk hot cream into beaten egg yolks. Return mixture to saucepan; stir in vanilla. Cook over medium heat, stirring constantly, until custard reaches 160°F and is thick enough to coat back of metal spoon (4 to 5 minutes). (Do not boil because egg yolks will curdle.) Refrigerate 8 hours or overnight. Remove truffle dessert from pan by lifting the aluminum foil. Remove aluminum foil. Slice truffle dessert with hot knife into 16 slices. Spoon about 1 tablespoon custard onto individual dessert plates; place slice of truffle dessert over custard. Garnish with finely chopped hazelnuts. **YIELD:** 16 servings.

Nutrition Information (1 serving): Calories 380; Protein 4g; Carbohydrate 26g; Fat 31g;
Cholesterol 145mg; Sodium 45mg.

Chocolate Caramel Fudge Sauce

A rich and creamy fudge sauce featuring milk chocolate chips, caramels and half-and-half.

Preparation time: 30 minutes • (pictured)

20 caramels, unwrapped

1 1/2 cups real milk
  chocolate chips

1/2 cup half-and-half

2 tablespoons
  LAND O LAKES® Butter

In 2-quart saucepan combine all ingredients. Cook over medium low heat, stirring often, until caramels and chocolate are melted and mixture is smooth (10 to 20 minutes). Serve warm over ice cream or cake. **YIELD:** 1 1/2 cups.

Nutrition Information (1 tablespoon): Calories 100; Protein 1g; Carbohydrate 12g; Fat 6g; Cholesterol 5mg; Sodium 40mg.

Flavored Coffees

The perfect way to end a delightful meal
— a cup of flavored coffee.

(pictured)

Weak Coffee
1 tablespoon coffee
3/4 cup (6 ounces) water*

Medium Coffee
2 tablespoons coffee
3/4 cup (6 ounces) water*

Strong Coffee
3 tablespoons coffee
3/4 cup (6 ounces) water*

For flavored coffees, start with strong brewed coffee.

* Use freshly drawn cold water; do not use softened water.

Irish Coffee: Stir in Irish whiskey and sugar to taste. Top with sweetened whipped cream.

Almond Coffee: Stir in almond flavored liqueur to taste. Top with sweetened whipped cream and toasted sliced almonds. For non-alcoholic Almond Coffee use medium brewed coffee. Stir in almond extract and sugar to taste. Top with sweetened whipped cream and toasted sliced almonds.

Mexican Coffee: Stir in coffee flavored liqueur to taste. Top with sweetened whipped cream; sprinkle with brown sugar and cinnamon.

Chocolate Coffee: Stir in chocolate flavored syrup and cream to taste.

Iced Coffee: Cool coffee; serve over ice. Stir in sugar, cream and/or milk to taste, if desired.

Coffee N' Cream: Stir in your favorite flavor ice cream to taste.

Coffee Condiments
To be used as condiments with hot brewed coffee: Chocolate curls, grated orange peel, orange slices, cinnamon sticks, sweetened whipped cream, brown sugar and your favorite liqueurs.

Spicy Whipped Cream
Serve dolloped on hot brewed coffee.

> **1 cup whipping cream**
> **2 tablespoons powdered sugar**
> **1/4 teaspoon cinnamon**
> **Dash nutmeg**

In chilled small mixer bowl beat chilled whipping cream at high speed, scraping bowl often, until soft peaks form. Continue beating, gradually adding powdered sugar, cinnamon and nutmeg, until stiff peaks form. **YIELD:** 1 1/2 cups.

Index